Your Photo on God's Fridge Door
101 Original Parables and Analogies for Today

Gordon S. Jackson

M Zion Ridge Press
Books Off the Beaten Path

Mt Zion Ridge Press LLC
295 Gum Springs Rd, NW
Georgetown, TN 37366

https://www.mtzionridgepress.com

ISBN 13: 978-1-955838-80-1

Published in the United States of America
Publication Date: December 15, 2023

Copyright: © Gordon S. Jackson 2023

Editor-In-Chief: Michelle Levigne
Executive Editor: Tamera Lynn Kraft

Cover art design by Tamera Lynn Kraft
Cover Art Copyright by Mt Zion Ridge Press LLC © 2023

The following entries were previously published as follows, and are excerpted with permission:

Entry 12, from *The God Who Blesses: 50 Reflections on Blessings and Blessedness* (Kharis Publishing: 2022), by Gordon S. Jackson

Entries 15, 29, 69 and 79 from *Be Thou My Vision: Light, Sight and the Christian Faith* (Crosslink: 2017), by Gordon S. Jackson

Entries 41 and 100 in *A Handbook for Discovering God's Will* (Navpress: 2008), by Gordon S. Jackson

Entries 36, 50 and 82 from *Jesus Does Stand-Up – And Other Satires* (Wipf and Stock: 2010), by Gordon S. Jackson.

Entries 3, 30, 42, 43, 46, 73, 74, 88, 94 and 101.in *Ninety Days of Difference: Devotionals for Village Schools International* (Kindle Direct Publishing: 2023), by Gordon S Jackson

"Though analogy is often misleading, it is the least misleading thing we have."

— *Samuel Butler*

Table of Contents

Introduction

You're on the right road. But it's late at night and you're driving through unfamiliar countryside and a succession of small villages. Even with the help of your car's headlights, it's not easy to see what lies ahead. The headlights are illuminating what lies immediately in front, giving you an accurate and trustworthy picture of reality. But what of the terrain lying 100 yards to the left or the right? You can have little idea of what lies outside your illuminated line of sight, such as a deer on a collision path with your car. You're making steady progress, but some extra lighting would make the journey easier, as you wonder what else is out there. And that is the point of this book: to provide one illustration after another that will better illuminate the road of your Christian journey.

Oh, there it is again… that metaphor of the Christian life as a journey. Philosopher and theologian Peter Kreeft says that "The image of life as a road is probably the single most popular image in the world's literature"[1] – and he might have added, the world's religions. As a result, however, the image is overworked and in need of either a sabbatical or full retirement. The trouble is, it's such a useful picture that we Christians keep using it. Same with our "Christian walk," our role as "ambassadors for Christ," or "fighting the good fight" and "running the race." These biblically grounded images were rich when Christians first used them. Now, because the concepts they represent are central to our theology, we keep using these phrases because they remain effective shorthand for what we want to say, clichéd though they may be.

By contrast, the illustrations in *God's Fridge Door* are fresh and original – which is how Jesus' illustrations and word pictures in His teaching would have struck His listeners. We too find those teaching techniques highly effective in our learning today. Whether we're talking about parables, analogies, similes, or metaphors, they all fit under the heading of figurative language. So, given how our Lord repeatedly invigorated His teaching with one word picture after another, it's not surprising that effective preachers, writers, and others who proclaim the gospel emulate Jesus' approach.

Admittedly, using figurative language in the church has its challenges. Even Jesus' disciples needed some of the parables explained to them. Debra and Ron Rienstra, in their book *Worship Words*, point out some limitations of using figurative speech. For example, "No human

---

[1] Peter Kreeft: *The Journey: A Spiritual Roadmap for Modern Pilgrims.*

language (even the precious and inspired words of the Bible) can fully describe the splendor and mystery of God." Every metaphor is inevitably incomplete. Another concern they identify is that "Metaphors can become distorted, bringing misleading implications with them."

However, used with care and with an awareness of their limitations, the language of images and parables, metaphors, and similes — figurative wording of every kind — can greatly enrich our understanding of God's Kingdom. All the more so if those images are new to us. As the Rienstras put it, "We need a healthy diet of images for a healthy faith life." And that is what *God's Fridge Door* seeks to provide.

~~~~~

First, though, some definitions would help. What do we mean when we talk about figurative language, analogies, metaphors, similes and parables?

Figurative language is an umbrella term, covering the other concepts we'll refer to. Dictionary.com says figurative language is "intended to create an image, association, or other effect in the mind of the listener or reader that goes beyond the *literal* meaning or expected use of the words involved." So a phrase like "light as a feather" is figurative speech. Think of it as creating an easily grasped picture for the person on the receiving end.

Analogy is a common rhetorical device to illustrate or expand someone's understanding of a concept. One grammar book defines it as "a comparison between two things alike in some respects, but dissimilar in others."[2] And Paula LaRocque, in *The Book on Writing*, says an analogy is "one of the most dependable devices for making difficult, unfamiliar, or technical material interesting and easy to understand. Analogies relate the unfamiliar to the familiar."

Analogies are especially helpful in trying to explain more abstract ideas or concepts. For example, how to describe to a six-year-old the idea of the Trinity? The old analogy that points to the three forms of water — liquid, solid, and gas — can help a child grasp at least an initial understanding of this mysterious concept.[3]

An analogy is subdivided into metaphors and similes. In a **metaphor**, the writer or speaker asserts something we know is a comparison but not something to be taken literally. So when Jesus says, "I am the bread of life,"

---

[2] E. Fletcher and W. Sceales: *High School English.*
[3] Admittedly, this is not a perfect analogy and one risks introducing the child to the heresy of modalism, a discussion of which is beyond the scope of this book. Still, for a six-year-old an imperfect ice/water/steam analogy is much more helpful than any attempt to explain the danger of modalism.

nobody understands that to mean that He is in fact a loaf of bread.[4] Instead, with the familiar image of bread in our minds, we better understand that He will sustain our need for spiritual food.

When Jesus told His disciples, "I am I am the way, the truth and the life," (Jn. 14:6) another of the seven "I am" statements in John's gospel, He gave them excellent direction for the ministries to which He had called them. The seven statements offer powerful metaphors or visual pictures:

- *I am the bread of life.* (Jn. 6:35)
- *I am the light of the world.* (Jn. 8:12)
- *I am the door of the sheep.* (Jn. 10:2)
- *I am the good shepherd.* (Jn. 10:11)
- *I am the resurrection and the life.* (Jn. 11:25)
- *I am the true vine.* (Jn. 15:1)

In a **simile** the writer or speaker explicitly likens one thing to another. Legendary Scottish poet Robbie Burns famously wrote:

O my love is like a red, red rose
That's newly sprung in June;
O my love is like the melody
That's sweetly played in tune.

We know that the object of his affection isn't literally a rose; she is *like* a rose, a flower that helps him affirm her beauty. Likewise, she is *like* a sweetly played melody, something inspiring or pleasing. The familiar images of the rose and the melody expand our understanding of his love.

There is little we need to say about **parables**. We know from Jesus' ministry that a parable is a lesson in story form that's intended to make a point about some aspect of God's Kingdom. Depending on how you count them, there are more than fifty parables recorded in the four gospels. There's much overlap between them, however, so again depending on how you keep score, the gospels contain about forty unique parables.

Scholars differ on whether a parable is intended to have only one main point. Some argue that two or more key lessons can be drawn from one story. There's no need to debate that issue here. However, we do need to beware of falling into the trap of allegorizing parables or other images, whether in Scripture or in this collection. The early church was prone to "over-reading" meaning into Jesus' parables. Well-intentioned though these efforts were, contemporary scholarship doesn't see allegorizing as a

---

[4] We get into complicated theological territory when we think of Jesus' institution of the Lord's supper, and His assertion that the bread is His body. Our concern for the present is what He said in John 6:35.

3

valid approach to interpreting these parables. This practice led to examples like this interpretation of the Good Samaritan by Origen, who lived about 185 to 254 (his exact dates are disputed):

> *The man who was going down is Adam.* <u>*Jerusalem*</u> *is paradise, and Jericho is the world. The robbers are hostile powers. The priest is the* <u>*Law*</u>*, the* <u>*Levite*</u> *is the* <u>*prophets*</u>*, and the Samaritan is Christ. The wounds are disobedience, the beast is the Lord's body, the [inn], which accepts all who wish to enter, is the* <u>*Church*</u>*. ... The manager of the [inn] is the head of the Church, to whom its care has been entrusted. And the fact that the Samaritan promises he will return represents the Savior's* <u>*second coming*</u>*.*

Instead of focusing on how we should analyze parables, our concern is the vivid imagery that Jesus used in telling these stories, some of which were quite short. What is common to His storytelling is Jesus' reliance on everyday imagery: scenes from agriculture, as with the parable of the sower (or the soils, as some people describe it); a lost coin; or the gripping tale of the Good Samaritan, tapping into the dangers of travel through bandit-infested territory as well as the deep divisions between Jews and Samaritans.

With *God's Fridge Door*, the emphasis is also on contemporary concepts to which readers can immediately relate: entries relating to computing, COVID 19, and heart transplants, among others, images not available to Jesus. And, of course, those decorations on our fridge doors.

~~~~~

As already noted, all figurative speech has its limits. Pushed to extremes, these devices can fail in their applicability and usefulness. The more literally we take them, the less effective they become. Burns no doubt expects us to focus on a freshly blooming rose, with a beautiful color and scent, and not on the thorns or the fact that the flower will soon fade away. When we take Jesus' words that He is the light of the world in a figurative sense, their power is obvious; we are not expected to take them literally and expect Him to replace the electricity in our home. Nor would we take literally the psalmist's assertion that "The Lord is my rock, my fortress." (Ps. 18:2) God is certainly *like* a rock and *like* a fortress, common themes in the psalms. Yet no sensible Christian for a moment believes God is *actually* a rock or a fortress. Likewise, as C.S. Lewis points out referring to the symbolic use of language in Scripture, "People who take these symbols literally might as well think that when Christ told us to be like doves, He meant that we were to lay eggs."[5]

---

[5] C. S. Lewis: *Mere Christianity.*

Jesus' initial hearers were smart enough to know the difference between figurative and literal speech. Whether they were listening to the parables for which He is famous, or analogies like the "I am" statements, He clearly thought that these devices were effective teaching tools and used them repeatedly. For instance, He is recorded ten times in Matthew's gospel as saying, "the Kingdom of Heaven is like....," as in "like a man who sowed good seed in his field," (Mt. 13:24) or "like a mustard seed." (Mt. 13:31) In each case, Jesus' use of a simile helps His listeners to more easily grasp a theological truth.

It was the same with parables. Although parables had long preceded Jesus as a teaching tool, He brought them into common usage in a way no one else has ever done. Our English language and Western culture are suffused with references to the good Samaritan, the prodigal son, and the lost sheep, for example. Even people who have minimal knowledge of Scripture use these shorthand labels to refer to some of Jesus' most memorable parables.

~~~~~

Now, to the material at hand. All Scripture references are from the *New International Version* of the Bible, except where noted otherwise. Then there is the issue of inclusive language. Some quotes use "man," "mankind" and so on when referring to people in general. These quotes reflect earlier usage which characterizes contemporary English less and less. In keeping with this volume's commitment to present all sources as accurately as possible, I have included these entries with their original wording.[6]

The metaphors, similes, and various modern-day parables that follow are each intended to illuminate some aspect of the Kingdom of God. A word of caution: don't get hung up on whether this illustration or that qualifies as a parable, metaphor or simile, or analyze any of these entries to death. Rather, take each at face value to learn how it might enrich some aspect of your faith.

My goal has been to provide an array of fresh insights into our faith via the window of analogies, with a few parables thrown into the mix. While it is possible you've encountered some of these ideas or comparable ones elsewhere, as far as I know all these entries are original.[7]

---

[6] The use of masculine pronouns to refer to God is done with due deference to concerns about inclusive language. Their use is not to assert that God is masculine. Where possible, attempts have been made to avoid masculine pronouns. But they have been included rather than resort to the heavy-handed artificiality of writing things like "We seek to know who God is, how God deals with us, and what God wants to characterize our life together as God's people." Elsewhere, quoted material using these pronouns is left unchanged, respecting the need to accurately present these sources.

[7] In a few cases I've reflected on historical incidents, with which you may be

How to use this book? You can dip into it wherever you want, reading the entries in whatever sequence you like. You may want to use these for your personal devotions. If you do, consider writing a brief response to each entry, especially in conjunction with other elements of your devotional time, such as prayer or Bible reading. If you are in Christian ministry, you may find these illustrations useful in preaching, teaching, or leading short devotionals.

These entries may occasionally interpret Scripture differently from your own understanding. If that occurs, feel free to rely on your own understanding of these Bible passages. But please don't let any such differences distract you from an entry's main point. But it's my hope that the insights that follow will enrich your own faith and help you in one way or another to share the marvelous riches of God's Kingdom with those whose lives you will touch.

Acknowledgements

The following friends read earlier versions of the entries that found their way into this anthology, and I am much in their debt for their critiques and suggestions: Malcolm de Kock, Jeff Haschick, Dia Maurer, Lisa McLean and Hans-Pieter Schragg. Their feedback was immensely helpful in shaping the final product.

I also need to thank Tamera Kraft, the Executive Editor at Mt Zion Ridge Press, for her enthusiastic support for this project, as well as Michelle Levigne, the Press' Editor in Chief for her rigorous editing of the manuscript. I am much in debt to each of them.

familiar, but given them what I trust is a fresh application to our faith.

1: Adaptability

I have become all things to all people so that by all possible means I might save some.

— 1 Corinthians 9:22

Researchers in Sydney, Australia, knew cockatoos were smart. But they were surprised to learn just how smart, as these observers reported in 2021. These birds had learned to open trash cans around the city in a quest for easy meals. The intriguing thing the researchers found was that initially one bird had learned the complex task of opening a bin. As CNN reported, "The bird has to pry open the lid with its beak, twist its neck sideways and hop onto …the edge of the bin, hold it open with its beak or foot, walk along the rim, and finally flip the lid open."[8]

Then, no less impressive, whichever cockatoo first developed this bin-opening technique, it began sharing it with others. Now the behavior has spread to various Sydney neighborhoods, as these birds enjoy a previously inaccessible source of food. How healthy this fast-food diet is for these birds is another matter.

The cockatoos present a textbook case of a species adapting to its environment. Regardless of your views on evolution, and how species have come into being, there's no doubt that every living thing knows a thing or two about adaptability. In fact, every creature has to adapt to its environment: temperatures, food and water supply, awareness of and protection from predators, and ensuring ways of producing offspring. Sometimes these adaptations are behavioral, as when penguins in Antarctica huddle together to generate warmth during their brutal winters.

Humans too have over time adjusted their bodies to their environment. Take for example Tibetans, who according to a *National Geographic* account, "thrive at altitudes where oxygen levels are up to forty percent lower than at sea level. Breathing air that thin would cause most people to get sick, but Tibetans' bodies have evolved changes in their body chemistry."[9]

Then there's the matter of what we could call "spiritual adaptability." Christians need to function in a wide array of "spiritual climates" or

---

[8] https://www.cnn.com/2021/07/22/australia/cockatoos-trash-can-study-intl-hnk-scli-scn/index.html. Accessed Sept. 4, 2023.
[9] *National Geographic*, July 2, 2014.

"spiritual environments." Some of these are hostile, some more benign. But like the apostle Paul we need to be aware of our surroundings and adjust our Christian witness accordingly. Paul stated this clearly in his letter to the Corinthians:

> To the Jews I became like a Jew, to win the Jews. To those under the law I became like one under the law (though I myself am not under the law), so as to win those under the law. To those not having the law I became like one not having the law (though I am not free from God's law but am under Christ's law), so as to win those not having the law. To the weak I became weak, to win the weak. I have become all things to all people so that by all possible means I might save some. (1 Cor. 9:20-22)

No, this wasn't some chameleon-like, wishy-washiness on his part. On the contrary, it was a Spirit-inspired adaptability intended to share the gospel with whomever he encountered.

Jesus too took different approaches when talking to different audiences. With the disciples and others genuinely seeking the Kingdom, He took a quite different tone compared with the pharisees and their hostility. Similarly, His adaptability showed in His dealings with Peter. These ranged from His tender forgiveness of this man who had denied Him three times, to the earlier harshness when Peter rebuked Jesus for saying He would need to die—and Jesus said, "Get behind me, Satan." (Mk. 8:33)

Likewise with us. We would talk quite differently about our faith to a Sunday School class of six-year-olds, compared with a water-cooler chat at work with that agnostic fellow from marketing. And that flexibility is a strength, not a weakness—just as those Australian cockatoos see their discovery of a new food source as a smart adaptation.

2: In Alien Territory

Do not love the world or anything in the world. If anyone loves the world, the love of the Father is not in him.

— 1 John 2:15

One attraction for many of the foreign service officers who serve US diplomatic interests abroad is the appeal of being able to go to "alien territory." Their postings, to embassies and consulates all around the world, include exotic tropical locations, vibrant and bustling European capitals, cities steeped in history and culture, and any number of places the rest of us would love to visit on vacation. Other officers, though, are placed in grim, hostile, and dangerous settings — places where crime runs rampant, the climate is awful, and both the government and populace are deeply hostile to the government the ambassadors represent.

Regardless of their placement, all need to deal with one fundamental fact. They are no longer at home. Even if they have been in a posting for years, they never feel entirely at ease. Things are different. The culture, the food, the sounds and smells, and the language usually are different from what they are accustomed to. Far more than those of us who travel for pleasure or work, these foreign service representatives living year-round in other countries need to show great flexibility and openness. Indeed, an ability to accommodate to their new setting is crucial to their success. In addition, a government needs representatives who can immerse themselves in their new settings without constantly pining for the familiarity of home.

These individuals may live something of a split identity: an English-speaking, westerner who is officially representing the US government in, for example, Brazil. Yet they never forget that above everything, they have come from and represent their home country; *that* is where their true identity lies. So, they need to accept the host culture on its terms, while never forgetting who they represent and why they are there. It's always a tricky balance, fitting in well enough locally to function well, but never fitting in so well that they compromise their ability to serve the government that sent them.

Christians too are in alien territory. And, if we take our faith seriously, we spend our lives trying to walk a fine line between being "in the world but not of the world." The apostle John warns us, "Do not love the world or anything in the world. If anyone loves the world, the love of the Father is not in him." (1 Jn. 2:15)

9

If we have become fully at ease in our earthly setting, we need seriously to question our usefulness and credibility as ambassadors. It is a peculiar thing: God has placed us in what is essentially alien territory, and we spend our lives trying to live in a world that we must at all costs avoid seeing as our true home. Like ambassadors, we need to remind ourselves constantly that we are on assignment; we don't in any final sense belong here. The Christian's true home is heaven.

That means living in whatever society we find ourselves with a temporary mindset; we are here only on assignment. But the longer we live in a place that we like, the more we may tend to forget the temporary nature of our posting. Quite how Christians and the church should relate to the culture in which they find themselves has been the subject of much argument and debate throughout Christianity's history.

It is important now and again for the church to take stock by asking, "What *is* the culture in which we live? And to what extent *are* we accommodating ourselves to that culture?" This is not to suggest for a moment that Christians should disengage from the world, and that Christians should flee from a hostile culture to our own enclaves, where we can huddle together for warmth against the secular chill. On the contrary, God appoints us to serve as "the salt of the earth" and "the light of the world." (Mt. 5:13-14) Ours is a mandate to engage the world, not to withdraw from it. How we do that is a task for every generation of Christians to learn anew, in whatever place they find themselves, as we seek to honor Paul's admonition: "Do not conform any longer to the pattern of this world ..." (Rom. 12:2)

Let's return to the picture of the ambassador or another foreign-service officer doing this delicate dance in an alien land. Good diplomats do an excellent job of relating to and understanding the local culture. They may well speak the local language, and thoroughly grasp local customs and culture. But they never forget that no matter how comfortable they become in this place away from home, it can never *be* their home—at least, not while they remain in the service of their sending country. Or, for Christians, their Lord.

3: The Ailing Centipede

The Lord is close to the brokenhearted and saves those who are crushed in spirit. The righteous person may have many troubles, but the Lord delivers him from them all....

— Psalm 34:18-19

A centipede was suffering from terrible gout; each of his one hundred feet caused him constant pain. He asked a friend what he could do. "Go and see Owl," said the friend. "He's the wisest of creatures and he'll know the answer."

So off hobbled the centipede and told Owl his problem. "Hmmm...," pondered Owl for a moment. "Well, here's what you should do. It won't completely cure the problem but it'll help. Become a mouse. That way, with only four legs, you'll have only one twenty-fifth of the pain."

Delighted, the centipede said, "That's a wonderful idea. So how do I become a mouse?"

Owl replied: "Can't help you there, I'm afraid; I'm only into policy, not implementation."

~~~~~

Owl may have seemed great on theory but weak on results. That gap between the two has a powerful application in our spiritual lives. Our theology *must* be applicable in the hustle and bustle of our everyday lives, amid the ethical conflicts, family tensions, and financial or health crises. Craig Barnes said, "One of my seminary teachers once cautioned that any theology that does not hold up in the emergency rooms of life must be held suspect."[10]

Just like Owl's proposed solution; his theory only *seemed* promising. The fact is, it was a lousy theory after all, unable to stand the test of reality, and certainly deserving to be held suspect, as the centipede soon learned.

Without morbidly dwelling on a possible catastrophe in your life (sudden death of a loved one, a grim medical diagnosis for yourself), how resilient do you think your theology or theories about God would be in such a crisis?

---

[10] Craig Barnes: *Yearning,*.

11

4: Are You All Right?

Let us examine our ways and test them, and let us return to the LORD.
— Lamentations 3:40

You're in a restaurant enjoying a leisurely meal with your family. Suddenly, the person at the table next to yours starts coughing violently, going red in the face and struggling to breathe properly. You get up and ask, as her family members are doing as well, "Are you all right?"

She nods yes, and the coughing begins to subside. She sips some water, and gasps, "Went down the wrong way." Her family is visibly relieved and after a few more sips of water the woman seems close to normal. You return to your seat.

You begin to think, though, what an odd question you had asked: "Are you all right?" Of course she wasn't; she was having an industrial strength coughing fit. And just as odd was her nodded answer, saying she was okay. Well, she wasn't.

What was happening here was an unspoken understanding of the difference between a "big picture all right" and a "small picture all right." You were in effect asking, "Are you about to die? Are emergency measures called for?" And she replied, "No, my overall health and wellbeing are fine, thank you; this is a minor hassle." It was obvious to both of you that at the "small picture" level she was by no means all right. The coughing and spluttering made that obvious. But it was an easy fix, and a few sips of water sorted her out. All was well.

This scenario presents a clear parallel to our spiritual wellbeing. If someone asked, "Are you all right, spiritually?" it would be helpful for you and the questioner to know at what level they were asking. Big picture? Or small picture? My big picture relationship with God may be fine, but because of a fight with my boss I'm down in the dumps today—and not exuding boundless Christian joy.

If, on the other hand, I'm having prolonged doubts about the very foundations of my faith, then my issue is far more serious than the spiritual equivalent of a coughing fit. Instead of a few sips of water, I probably need to check in with the Great Physician Himself. More than anyone, He knows my needs. And when He asks, "Are you all right?" He already knows the answer and is waiting to hear my response.

5: "As It Were" — A Speculation

And they saw the God of Israel: and there was under his feet as it were a paved work of a sapphire stone, and as it were the body of heaven in his clearness.
— *Exodus 24:10*, King James Version

The context for this verse is that Aaron and the elders of Israel accompany Moses to the foot of the mountain, which he and Joshua will soon ascend — and where Moses goes on to be alone with God for forty days. The verse also tells us something quite extraordinary: this group got to see the God of Israel. Commentators note that this must have been a partial vision or insight into God's glory, because elsewhere we're told that seeing God face to face would mean death. As God says a few chapters later, "you cannot see my face, for no one may see me and live." (Ex. 33:20)[11]

Besides the special experience this group had in their encounter with God, something else stands out in the way the *King James* translation treats this verse: the two back-to-back uses of the phrase "as it were..." We have "... *as it were* a paved work of a sapphire stone" and "... *as it were* the body of heaven." Like any of us who have seen something truly astonishing or breathtaking, which we then try to describe to someone else, we find ourselves struggling for adequate words. Perhaps you've experienced the exquisite beauty of the Grand Canyon or another equally overwhelming landscape. Or maybe you've just heard the most sublime piece of music. Trying to share that experience with someone else proves impossible. You realize how limited is your vocabulary and end up saying it was "like this or that," or "it was as if." You might as well tell your listeners, "Well, I guess you just had to be there."

So it was with those described in the verse above. The best they could come up with was that God's presence was "as if" He was standing on sapphire. And this sapphire was so splendid, so awe-inspiring that it was "like" the body of heaven. Clearly, the writer is grasping here. If we assume the writer is Moses, this is the best he can do. But how *can* you describe such moments?

---

[11]In verse 11 of this chapter we read that "The Lord would speak to Moses face to face, as one speaks to a friend." While this description testifies to the unique intimate relationship Moses had with God, even he could not have experienced the full glory of God's presence.

~~~~~

And now, the speculation…

One of those elders heads back to his tent, dumbstruck by what he has seen. For days, he keeps this to himself, hoping Moses will return from the mountain and help him and the others understand this experience. But as Moses seems to have vanished, he can't contain himself any longer. So he tries describing to his family what he experienced: "Well, it was kind of like I saw God, and He was standing on this incredible sapphire pavement, as it were."

And the wife responds in disbelief, "You saw *God*. Are you *sure*?"

"Believe me, I'm sure—I've never seen anything like it before. All of us, we were terrified."

One of the children: "Why can't we see God?"

"Well, we can't all see God."

Another child: "That's not fair, Daddy. I want to see God too."

The wife: "And why should only men get to see God?"

"I'll tell you what," said the dad: "how about I talk to some of the other elders and Aaron. Maybe we could make a statue or something that reminds us of God. What do you think?"

The first child: "Yeah, maybe a bull, like the Egyptians worship—or a calf; that would be cuter."

The dad responds, "Yes, that way we could all see God, as it were."

14

6: Baboons and Pumpkins

Indeed, it is easier for a camel to go through the eye of a needle than for someone who is rich to enter the Kingdom of God.

— Luke 18:25

If you're troubled by baboons wreaking havoc on your farm or garden, supposedly[12] a sure-fire way to get rid of them is as follows. Set out a pumpkin with a small hole, just big enough for the animal's hand to go through. Then wait.

Eventually an opportunistic baboon will find the pumpkin and put its hand in to get the seeds. Greedily, the animal will grasp a handful of seeds, only to find that it now cannot withdraw its seed-filled fist. Its desire for the seeds will, again supposedly, override its desire for freedom, and will sit there, frustrated and trapped. The animal is then at your mercy to dispose of as local laws permit.

How like us. We grasp what we cannot keep, like the rich young ruler in Luke 18, who so valued his wealth that he declined Jesus' offer of the true freedom that would come from following Him. It's not only wealth that can entrap us. Maybe we're so tied to our career that we resist God's call to ministry, and the full freedom and joy that would await us there.

"Let go," says God. "Trust me," while we persist in holding onto a bunch of pumpkin seeds.

---

[12] Please note the word "supposedly"—the author has not empirically verified this strategy.

7: Banishment

I, John, your brother and companion in the suffering and Kingdom and patient endurance that are ours in Jesus, was on the island of Patmos because of the word of God and the testimony of Jesus.

— Revelation 1:9

John was in exile on the island of Patmos when he received his apocalyptic Revelation, which now is the last book in the Bible. He was presumably banished there as part of a growing persecution of the young church. Although his freedom of movement was curtailed, his conditions were unlikely to have been as severe as if he were imprisoned. Unlike Paul, who was quite familiar with the inside of jails, John had it relatively easy. William Barclay says in his commentary on Revelation, "People so banished were not personally ill-treated and were not confined in prison on their island but were free to move within its narrow limits."

Still, John was limited in what he could do in his situation, one that many of us might relate to. We may be experiencing what we'd be justified in regarding as our own kind of banishment. We may have put our career on hold to take care of an elderly parent, or a child with a serious chronic illness. Or we may have sustained severe injuries in an accident that have put us out of commission for a prolonged period. Yet again, we may see ourselves more in a spiritual banishment, where we feel we're in limbo in our faith, stuck in a place where nothing especially bad is happening but we're not able to grow spiritually, either.

However we might experience banishment, we can be assured that God has neither abandoned nor forgotten us. As Oswald Chambers says, "All your circumstances are in the hands of God; therefore never think it strange concerning the circumstances you are in."[13] Whether those circumstances rise to the level of what you see as banishment, remember that God works through you no matter your situation. It was while he was on Patmos, cut off from the young church in Jerusalem, that John received his stirring vision; it was from prison that Paul wrote several of the letters that now instruct and inspire Christians two millennia later.

Even though you may currently view yourself as being constrained in some unwelcome way, God never is. Nor has He forgotten to comfort, sustain and use those of His people who are.

---

[13] Oswald Chambers: *My Utmost for His Highest*, Nov. 7.

8: A Beard or Not a Beard?

Jesus said to him, "I do not say to you seven times, but seventy times seven."
– Matthew 18:22, Revised Standard Version

Let's say I have a thousand hairs, neatly groomed, on my face. Presumably you will agree that I have a beard. Now let's say I have four hairs on my chin. A beard? Surely not. Once again, I assume you agree.

Okay, how about 772 hairs? Also a beard? Good, you're still with me. Well, what about twelve hairs? Is that a beard yet? Nope.

By now, you can guess where this is going: At some point I'm going to force you to admit that fifty hairs, for example, constitute a beard, but forty-nine do not. Or maybe it's sixty and fifty-nine that constitute the cut-off. The point is, I'm forcing you to choose a precise point on a continuum, comparable to asking exactly where on a black-white continuum does grey begin and end.

In other words, asking "How many hairs do you need to make a beard?" is a question without an answer. Not unlike Peter's question about how many times he should forgive. Is it seven? Rabbinic teaching was that one should forgive one's brother three times. So Peter is probably trying to impress Jesus by doubling that number, and adding yet another "forgiveness" just to be sure. Yet Jesus' answer of "until seventy times seven" (Mt. 18:22)[14] is His way of saying you've asked a question without an answer. "Forgive as many times as you need to," is what He's saying. He's not literally saying seventy-seven times,[15] after which you can stop forgiving. It is noteworthy that Jesus follows this encounter by telling the parable of the man who is indebted to a king for a huge amount, which is forgiven after the debtor's passionate pleading. But then the man goes out and demands a paltry amount that is owed to him.

Tying His answer and this parable together therefore makes Peter's question look silly in the light of the forgiveness we receive from God. Rather, the bigger picture here is that God's love doesn't lend itself to precise counting or measuring. As William Barclay comments on this passage, "[T]here is no reckonable limit to forgiveness."[16]

---

[14] This is the more familiar *The King James Version* wording.
[15] This is how the *NIV* translates this number. However, the significance remains the same.
[16] William Barclay: *The Daily Study Bible: Matthew vol. 2.*

And speaking of counting, the fact that the hairs on your head are numbered is an indication of God's love for you, not the focus of some angelic accountant assigned to hair counting. (Heads or beards, for that matter.)

9: Bewildered, Not Lost

God has said, "Never will I leave you; never will I forsake you."
– Hebrews 13:5

The frontiersman Daniel Boone was once asked if he'd ever been lost. His response: "I can't say I was ever lost, but I was bewildered once for three days."

Same for Christians. Times will come when we may feel lost, disoriented, confused in a dense forest and see no way out. It's okay at these times to feel bewildered. But it's crucial that we offset that bewilderment with the assurance that God is always with us. After all, "God has said, 'Never will I leave you; never will I forsake you.'" (Heb. 13:5)

Yes, we may be bewildered or perplexed, or even downright angry with God for our current circumstances and feel abandoned. But never should we see ourselves as lost.

10: The Big Game

But about that day or hour no one knows, not even the angels in heaven, nor the Son, but only the Father.

— Matthew 24:36

You're heading home after work, eager to watch the Big Game on TV. You've recorded it and carefully avoided the news to avoid a "spoiler" experience of learning the outcome prematurely.

About five miles from home, you make an unexpected connection between the recording you're about to watch and, of all things, Jesus' second coming. The outcome of the game, you realize, has already been decided. You don't know how long the game will last but you do know that your team either won or lost; nothing you do can change the result.

So too with Jesus' return; that outcome likewise has already been decided. You don't know how long we'll have to wait to see that divine "final play." Even Jesus didn't know the hour of His return: "But about that day or hour no one knows, not even the angels in heaven, nor the Son, but only the Father." (Mt. 24:36)

We can have no doubts, however, who will emerge as the winner.

11: The Blank Check Exercise

"Test me in this," says the LORD *Almighty, "and see if I will not throw open the floodgates of heaven and pour out so much blessing that there will not be room enough to store it."*

– Malachi 3:10

~~~~~

My best asking falls immeasurably short of my Father's giving.
– Streams in the Desert, devotional readings

Many of us receive a steady stream of financial offers in the mail, for this credit card or that, offers of wondrous benefits for opening a checking account with Bank X, or if you're approaching 65, a flood of ads for Medicare supplements.

However, imagine that you got an envelope with a return address indicating it was from God Himself. You open it, and the cover letter tells you that as a matter of sheer, undeserved grace, God is giving you a blank check. All you have to do is fill in the amount and take it to your bank and cash it. Suspicious, you phone your bank manager who—to your surprise—tells you, "Yes, we've had several of these come through already. This is perfectly legit. Bring it in and we'll take care of it." Then, she adds, "God's credit is good; don't worry."

First, though, you need to fill in the amount. What will you enter? How will you decide? On the one hand, you don't want to short-change God or insult Him by entering something like $17.58. Nor do you want to be greedy. Entering $76 million would be brazenly exploitative of His grace. So what amount *will* you choose?

Before you get your hopes up, return to reality and accept that this scenario is far from likely. What is already a reality, though, is that God assures us of as much grace as we will need. Speaking in the context of his "thorn in the flesh," Paul says that God told him, "My grace is sufficient for you, for my power is made perfect in weakness." (2 Cor. 12:9)

Maybe that blank check idea isn't so far-fetched after all. Take it a step further, and ask, what if there'd be a new blank check *every* morning (not unlike the manna and quail that sustained the desert-traipsing Israelites)? What do you need today's check for?

Time to head to the bank....

12: The Blessed Experience

For where your treasure is, there your heart will be also.

— *Luke 12:48*

Honor Gilbert, writing about the value of keeping a spiritual journal, described a man who went overboard, so fixated on one entry that he kept trying to re-live what for him was a spiritually profound moment. He wrote down a vivid account of his experience, and frequently re-read it and fixated on it. Then, Gilbert writes, "One day he rushed down to his wife in great distress, 'The mice have eaten my blessed experience,' he cried."[17]

~~~~

This poor man had three problems. First, he kept looking backwards in his faith, not forward. He should have heeded the wisdom of Paul Tournier, who said, "The Holy Spirit is always calling us to look forward, not back."[18]

Second, his was a self-absorbed faith, focusing on *his* experience, and what God had done for *him*. He was living out a Christian experience so narrowly defined that he precluded whatever else God had in store for him. He had done exactly what Oswald Chambers warned against: "not to make a fetish of your rare moments."[19]

The third problem, understandably, was getting rid of the mice.

---

[17] Quoted in Edward England: *Keeping a Spiritual Journal*.
[18] Paul Tournier: *The Adventure of Living*.
[19] Oswald Chambers: *My Utmost for His Highest*, April 25.

22

13: Blind Skiing

Trust in the LORD with all your heart and lean not on your own understanding; in all your ways submit to him, and he will make your paths straight.

— Proverbs 3:5-6

Mike May was blinded in both eyes following a chemical explosion when he was three. Then, in 2000, aged forty-six, he regained some sight in one eye following pioneering stem cell surgery by a San Francisco ophthalmologist. Robert Kurson's book, *Crashing Through*, grippingly tells May's story, of his life as someone totally blind, the risk he took in undergoing the surgery, and the restoration of vision but with mixed results. May had never let his blindness hold him back in life. Such was his sense of adventure that he took up downhill skiing, among other activities. He became so proficient, following a sighted skier, that he set a speed record for a blind skier of sixty-five miles per hour and also earned three bronze medals in the 1984 winter Paralympics.[20]

The sheer courage May displays throughout his life is noteworthy in its own right. But our focus here is instead on the role of the sighted skier leading a blind man down a ski slope at sixty-five miles per hour, and the absolute trust the blind skier must place in the sighted one—not only to have good intentions but also a level of skill that requires the leader to anticipate every move for two skiers.

May's lack of physical sight parallels our limited spiritual vision. We have some idea regarding the terrain of the journey on which God has invited us. Let's assume it's a road trip, most likely something more familiar to all of us. Sitting beside us as we drive, He says: "There's a sharp curve ahead, slow down." We do. Later, He says, "There's a major traffic snarl ahead on the freeway; we can avoid it by taking the next exit and going on Route 38." Once again we follow God's direction, trusting both His good intentions and His knowledge of the road, its conditions, and possible hazards.

But later God says, "Okay, we're now back on the freeway. The limit here is sixty-five. Get up to that speed."

You do. Then God says, "Now I want you to close your eyes and keep driving."

---

[20] This paragraph is taken from Gordon S. Jackson's *Be Thou My Vision: Light, Sight and the Christian Faith.*

You hesitate, then you hear the words, "Eyes closed. Trust Me."

Then God adds, "We're about to enter Montana. The limit here is seventy-five to eighty. Eyes still closed, yes? You still doing okay?"

14: Bob Beamon's Moment

I am the LORD, the God of all mankind. Is anything too hard for me?
— Jeremiah 32:27

Bob Beamon was an American athlete who entered the 1968 Mexico Olympics as a favorite to take the gold in the long jump. While he was up against stiff opposition, including two gold medalists, he had won twenty-two of the twenty-three events he'd participated in that year. He barely made it into the finals, however, after overstepping on his first two runs. Then came the moment, on October 18 that year, that propelled him into athletics history, and added a new word to the English vocabulary: Beamonesque.

In a sport where records were achieved in inches or fractions of inches, Beamon's gold-medal leap shattered the previous record by just under twenty-two inches, a world record that stood for twenty-three years. The Olympic record still stands. So does the word in sports jargon: Beamonesque, meaning, as one writer put it, "an athletic feat so dramatically superior to previous feats that it overwhelms the imagination."[21]

So it is at times with our life of faith. They may be instances of perfectly natural events, like Beamon's jump, that are so unexpected that they have at least a hint of the miraculous about them. Or they may be things that we can explain only as miracles. Maybe it was a radical healing, quite unexpected—and unexplained—by the medical community. Or perhaps it was a set of circumstances defying all human odds that led to a positive outcome.

Whatever the incident that "overwhelmed the imagination," however, we need to respond in at least two ways. The first should obviously be gratitude to God. The second should be a recognition that a problem with miracles (or their close relatives, what we could call turbocharged coincidences) is that we think we're so special we're entitled to miracle-level treatment and look for an encore performance.

Rather, a balanced approach calls for a handle on two realities. The Anglican Church in Egypt has a two-campus theological college, based jointly in Cairo and Alexandria. The school began in 2005 and its founding document said it aspired to produce graduates who lived "in anticipation

---

[21] https://everything-everywhere.com/beamonesque-bob-beamons-incredible-olympic-record/. Accessed Sept. 4, 2023.

Gordon S. Jackson

of miracle and acceptance of constraint." We must live then in the unhesitating confidence that at any moment God could bring a miracle to bear on our circumstances. Simultaneously, though, we ought also to live with the "acceptance of constraint" of a real world, marked today by the ordinary, the routine, the predictable. Unlike October 18, 1968.

26

15: Borrowed Light

You are the light of the world ... let your light shine before men.
— Matthew 5:14-15

We can read Jesus' statement in Matthew three ways:
- *We* are the light of the world.
- We are the *light* of the world.
- We are the light of the *world*.

Whether the emphasis is on our role, what that role consists of, or the object of our role, it is clear from Jesus' Sermon on the Mount that He has high expectations of the part we are to play in bringing about the Kingdom of God. But lest we are tempted even for a moment to think we are a big deal, we need to recall that the light we reflect to the world is not our own; it is a borrowed light.

As William Barclay says of these two verses in Matthew's gospel, Jesus "was using an expression which was quite familiar to the Jews who heard it [from Him] for the first time. They themselves spoke of Jerusalem as 'a light to the Gentiles,' and a famous rabbi was often called 'a lamp of Israel.'" He continues:

> Of one thing the Jews were very sure — people never kindled their own light. Jerusalem was indeed a light to the Gentiles, but "God lit Israel's lamp." The light with which the nation or the people of God shone was a borrowed light. It must be so with the Christian. It is not the demand of Jesus that we should ... produce our own light. We must shine with the reflection of His light.[22]

All of our sight depends on external light sources; we never generate the light that illuminates our way ahead. Likewise, when non-Christians see in us "the light of the world," it is never our own light but a reflection of Christ's.

For both our physical and spiritual needs, we are totally dependent on God-given light; we have nothing of our own to illuminate our own journeys, or those of others. To the extent we seem to emit any light of our

---

[22] William Barclay, *The Daily Study Bible: Matthew*, vol. 1.

own, this too arises not from any inherent merit of our own; we are merely mirrors, reflecting what comes from the Light of the World Himself.

16: Breaking Story

"For my thoughts are not your thoughts, neither are your ways my ways," declares the LORD.

— Isaiah 55:8

Imagine your local TV station is covering a hostage situation in an elementary school on the north side of town. Apparently, a man with an automatic weapon is holding thirty-two second-graders captive. That's more or less all that is known.

The station is covering it live and the reporter on the scene and the anchor tell you what little they know and they assure you they are on top of this breaking story. Most news stories are an account of what has already happened. They are "past tense" stories: a fire gutted an apartment early this morning; a driver lost control of his car on ice and died after slamming into a tree; the state legislature approved the controversial bill on family leave.

But prolonged live coverage, as with our hostage example, provides the media with little new information to report moment by moment. Determined to stick with the story, however, even though there's in fact nothing new to tell, the anchor and the reporter will go back and forth, and the hapless reporter keeps coming up with yet another way of saying, "We have a hostage situation and there's nothing more I can tell you." The grim-faced anchor will also endlessly echo and restate what's already known.

Yet plenty may be unfolding behind the scenes, out of view of TV station's camera and beyond the reporter's knowledge. Perhaps negotiators are talking with the hostage taker. Or maybe the hostage taker has shot himself but law enforcement wants to wait until they are certain it will be safe to enter the building. Just because the TV reporter sees nothing happening doesn't mean that is the case.

Such a "no-news" situation has a parallel in our Christian lives — but in a positive way precisely the opposite of a hostage situation that is commanding continuous coverage. For God's story is always unfolding even when it seems there's nothing new to report. As Reuben Welch said, "With God, even when nothing is happening, something is happening."[23] In ways we cannot see, God is always active, always accomplishing His

---

[23] Quoted in https://www.drjamesdobson.org/newsletters/dr-james-dobsons-august-2017-newsletter. Accessed Sept. 4, 2023.

purposes.

That includes God's overarching work of establishing His Kingdom, on a cosmic scale, as well as at the individual level. Regarding our individual lives, Eugene Peterson reflects on his duties as a pastor: "We are always coming in on something that is already going on... Always we are dealing with what the risen Christ has already set in motion."[24]

Therefore, he adds, "In every visit, every meeting I attend, every appointment I keep, I have been anticipated. The risen Christ got there ahead of me." He imagined how, for example, "'...He is going before you to 1020 Emmorton Road; there you will see Him, as He told you.' Later in the day it will be, 'He is risen, ... He is going before you to St. Joseph's Hospital; there you will see Him, as He told you.'"

Similarly, Dawson Trotman, the founder of the Navigators Bible reading ministry, encouraged people to find out what God was already doing and then jump on board.

Think what you have lined up today: a meeting with the marketing committee, a doctor's appointment about that chronic back ache, a parent-teacher conference late this afternoon. Whatever it is, imagine Christ having gone before you. Realize too that He has been at work, preparing the ground for your arrival. In other words, if you assume that when it comes to God's unfolding story there's nothing to report, you are completely misreading the situation. For "With God, even when nothing is happening, something is happening."

---

[24] Eugene H. Peterson: *Living the Message*, Sept. 18.

17: Carried Home

Even to your old age and gray hairs I am he, I am he who will sustain you.
I have made you and I will carry you…
— Isaiah 46:4

Softball player Sara Tucholsky, from Western Oregon University, had just hit her first ever home run and was rounding first base in the contest against home team Central Washington University, in April 2008. That's when she twisted her knee so badly that she couldn't continue; she had torn her ACL. The rules of the game prevented her teammates or coach from helping her.

Mallory Holtman, one of the CWU players, asked the officials if her team could help the injured opponent make it to home plate. That was permitted, so Holtman and teammate Liz Wallace carried their opponent around the remaining bases, ensuring she touched each of the remaining bases, and so securing Tucholsky's moment of glory — and their own.

The incident received international attention as an example of generosity of spirit in sports. A poster showing the three players hobbling toward home plate was distributed to schools as a model of good sportsmanship.

~~~~~

Ugo Betti, an Italian judge and author, said: "To believe in God is to know that all the rules will be fair and that there will be wonderful surprises."[25] Like that softball contest in 2008. As we engage in the game, we discover we can't even make it to first base without incapacitating ourselves. The rules leave us in despair; there's no going any further. We're in acute pain and that dream of getting a home run is over.

Then comes the surprise, the astonishing, unmerited, and costly move: God steps in and says, "It's okay; I make the rules here. I'll carry you home."

---

[25] Quoted in Gordon S. Jackson: *Quotes for the Journey, Wisdom for the Way.*

18: Checking the Gauges

You need to persevere so that when you have done the will of God, you will receive what he has promised.

— Hebrews 10:36

You're seven hours into your long road trip. Boredom set in long ago. But being an experienced driver, you haven't forgotten the crucial importance of checking your speedometer every now and then so you haven't let your speed drift fifteen or twenty miles per hour above the legal limit. You also glance at your fuel gauge; still a third of a tank, which will easily get you to your destination tonight. Also, because it's a hot day and you are halfway up a steep mountain pass, you glance at the temperature gauge as well. Likewise, no problems.

Although he predated the automobile era by more than three centuries, Francis de Sales (1567-1622) would have understood the importance of checking the gauges. He was a nobleman who, like his namesake St. Francis of Assisi, forsook his position in society and became a priest. Eventually he was appointed bishop of Geneva. He said, "Twice or thrice a day, look to see if your heart is not disquieted about something; and if you find that it is, take care forthwith to restore it to calm."[26] Not a bad suggestion, that.

What might be the gauges on your spiritual dashboard that merit checking as you go through today? Your irritation level? Your resentment gauge? Your self-loathing or anxiety measures? And depending on the readings you notice, take whatever steps are needed to "restore calm" as you continue your spiritual road trip.

---

[26] Quoted in *Streams in the Desert,* devotional readings, Oct. 12.

19: Christians: An Indicator Species

But you are a chosen race, a royal priesthood, a holy nation, a people for his own possession, that you may proclaim the excellencies of him who called you out of darkness into his marvelous light.

— 1 Peter 2:9

An "indicator species," if you're not familiar with the term, is one that's especially sensitive to the environmental conditions in a given location. An over-simplified example is the canary in the early, lower-tech days of coal mining: the poor creature died if lethal gases were present in the mine and which people couldn't smell. The death of a canary told the miners to leave. *Now.*

These days, we know that frogs serve a similar warning role if environmental conditions around them change significantly for the worse. Toxic chemicals, for example, can severely cut their population, when we humans haven't yet noticed any changes around us.

On the other hand, some creatures, like the platypus, can give more cheerful news: this odd critter is "typically one of the first species to return to a water body when the quality starts to improve,"[27] according to one authority.

So what can the "indicator species" concept teach Christians? Whether we know it or not, people are watching us and our responses to the world around us. We should be serving as an early-warning system, alerting others to anything that's harmful to our common environment. Do we signal that our society's hyper-individualism isn't what God has in mind for all of us? Same with our society's obsession with celebrities, looking cool, or having lots of toys? Frog-like, we should be filling that warning role, telling our society that our relentlessly consumer-driven way of life is polluting the pond, and moving us farther away from the kind of thriving, God-centered life that our heavenly Father desires.

But there's a positive role too. Like the platypus, we can offer hope by pointing out the clean, healthy water we've found in the gospel message, and tell our neighbors, "It's good; jump in and join us."

---

[27] https://www.theswimguide.org/2018/02/05/indicator-species. Accessed Sept. 4, 2023.

20: Church from the Sidelines

We hear that some among you are idle and disruptive. They are not busy;
they are busybodies.

— 2 Thessalonians 3:11

~~~~~

[T]he church has been compared to a soccer game, with a handful of
exhausted players doing all the running, surrounded by experts — many of them
desperately in need of exercise — who know everything they are doing wrong.

— Emanuel Oladipo

Which are you: exhausted player or expert on the sidelines? Admittedly, Oladipo has posed an unfair choice, offering us a false dichotomy. If you're living a healthy Christian life, you may be neither an exhausted player nor a sideline critic.

But if you are currently on the sidelines, it may be that you are burned out, having failed to follow the rule one pastor had. He said nobody in the church should have two jobs until everyone has one. Dedicated as you were, you chaired the church council, taught in the Sunday School, oversaw the stewardship campaigns for the last seven years, and so on. You're exhausted. Or perhaps you're unable to serve directly because of your health or your work commitments. You may even be away for extended periods because of military service.

Instead, Oladipo likely has his eye on yet another category of "non-players," those who have no real interest in getting on the field anyway. They fit the description of a critic as someone who comes down the hill after the battle and shoots the wounded. No doubt Paul had this category of church people in mind when he told the Thessalonians: "We hear that some among you are idle and disruptive. They are not busy; they are busybodies." (2 Thess. 3:11)

Every pastor will no doubt encounter those who are idle in their affiliation with the church. Worse are those who are both "idle and disruptive." A wise pastor will (1) identify these individuals, and (2) try to neutralize their negative impact. On the other hand, a pastor should also be attentive to those who are so immersed in church life that they're running ragged, to the point of exhaustion.

A healthy church should consist of people living balanced lives. Wise leadership is alert to imbalance, for individuals and the congregation or parish as a whole. It may be time to sub out some of those exhausted players staggering around the field and bring into play some folks who thus far have been content to sit on the sidelines taking shots at the wounded.

21: The Church as a Spiritual Toxic Waste Dump

If we confess our sins, he is faithful and just and will forgive us our sins and purify us from all unrighteousness.

– 1 John 1:9

If you don't see your church as a toxic waste dump, perhaps you should. You'll more easily grasp this idea if you're Catholic, especially if you regularly go to confession. That's because that small, private, and sacred space to the side of the sanctuary is a veritable dumping ground for sin and guilt. One parishioner after another has poured out one wrongdoing after another to one priest after another. Those who are genuinely repentant leave with hearts forgiven, and sins lying abandoned on the confessional floor. (Orthodox Christians tend to rely on confessing either to a priest or another mature Christian filling the role of a "spiritual father.")

Those of us who are Protestants may on rare occasions try the equivalent exercise expected of our Catholic brothers and sisters and find our own confessor. Normally, though, we are expected to go it alone, confessing our sins either in our private devotions or perhaps at a point in our church's worship service that specifically provides for confession of sin. Yet however we do so, confession should be an integral part of our Christian walk. As the apostle John writes, "If we confess our sins, He is faithful and just and will forgive us our sins and purify us from all unrighteousness." (1 Jn. 1:9)

One rule in avoiding clutter in your home or office is, "Don't put it down, put it away." Everything should have its place. If you're a Catholic, you already have a place provided for you: the confessional at church, where you can dump your sins and receive absolution. But if you're a Protestant, you must find or make a place. Perhaps you can rely on a time of confession in your church service. If that's not an option, come up with a place of your own.

No matter your faith tradition, your spiritual health is undermined by unconfessed sin. Either find the spiritual toxic waste dump nearest to you or check in directly with God. Like the father in the story of the prodigal son, He too is waiting to hear the words, " Father, I have sinned against heaven and against you." (Lk. 15:21) He is always ready to listen. And to forgive.

22: Cleaning the Whiteboard of Your Soul

Even though your sins are bright red, they will be as white as snow.
— Isaiah 1:18

If you've ever used an aging white board, you know that it can be difficult to completely erase what you've written. No matter how much you rub the eraser across the surface, it seems there's always a residue of unwanted ink.

Then you remember to reach for the bottle of dry erase cleaner, which you spray on the board and after wiping it across the surface the residue magically disappears.

Sort of like our souls: no matter how hard we try to clean ourselves up, there's always that stuff we can't remove. That's when we to turn, once again, to God's promise, which even specifies the color: "Even though your sins are bright red, they will be as white as snow." (Is. 1:18)

23: Compliant Patients and the Great Physician

Jesus said, "It is not the healthy who need a doctor, but the sick.... I have not come to call the righteous, but sinners."

— Matthew 9:12-13

Few things irritate doctors more than patients who are not compliant. Patients who ignore their doctors' instructions either delay or prevent their recovery, possibly making their condition even more difficult to treat in the future. Another irritant is patients who don't tell the doctor all he or she needs to know. Perhaps they hold back out of embarrassment or shame, or they're tired of their doctor repeatedly reminding them to quit smoking, lose weight, or cut down on alcohol. In brief, doctors obviously cannot diagnose and then prescribe properly if their patients don't cooperate.

We can expect similar difficulties when approaching the Great Physician, the ultimate specialist in dealing with sicknesses of the soul: "Jesus said, 'It is not the healthy who need a doctor, but the sick... I have not come to call the righteous, but sinners.'" (Mt. 9:12-13)

He's always on call, doesn't require insurance, and unlike our regular doctors, is all-knowing. Still, Jesus wants us to be honest with Him, if necessary, baring our souls to reveal what we might hide from others. Pierre Wolff says, "When I need a doctor's care, I show him my wounds. I do not hide them and show him only what is healthy. Refusing to call hatred and resentment by their real names would be hiding my wounds from the Lord."[28] Or whatever it is that is wounding your spirit.

---

[28] Source unknown.

24: The Crack

For the wages of sin is death, but the gift of God is eternal life in Christ Jesus our Lord.

— Romans 6:23

Kintsugi is an artistic technique, by which the artist binds a crack in a piece of crockery, for example, with lacquer, and covers the joins with silver or gold. And it's a technique that is in vogue in the West, according to a March 2021 report in *The Economist*.

The magazine also tells of an artist who reflects on *kintsugi* from a Christian perspective. Makoto Fujimura, who was born in Boston but grew up in Japan, has won acclaim internationally for his work. The article quotes Fujimura as saying that like a broken piece of pottery, "We are wretched, broken fragments of what was once beautiful." Then, he adds, thanks to Jesus "our fissures become filled with gold." He insists on using expensive materials in his work, reflecting what the magazine says is "a frank delight in artistic abundance, even extravagance." In his book titled *Art and Faith*, Fujimura justifies this extravagance by saying, "As God's creation is sumptuous and even excessive, so must our responses be."

The parallel for Christians is two-fold. First, there is the recognition that we are broken individuals. Second, there's the recognition that not only is our healing or restoration accomplished by Jesus, it is accomplished by the very best means possible. God engaged in no second-rate measures to restore us to Himself; no shoddy, cheap materials for God the artist. Similarly, it's appropriate that anyone looking at a formerly scarred or fractured Christian is now drawn immediately to the *kintsugi*, the costly repair and its brilliance, reflecting the extravagance of its Maker and Repairer.

Gordon S. Jackson

25: Cricket and Joining Jesus' Team

My Kingdom is not of this world. If it were, My servants would fight to prevent my arrest by the Jewish leaders. But now my Kingdom is from another place.

— John 18:36

Peter Kreeft is one smart fellow. He's a professor of philosophy at Boston College and an author of more than seventy books—leading him to be described as one of the most widely read Christian authors of our time. But he has his limits: "Like most Americans, I simply cannot understand how the English can possibly be fascinated with cricket, so I just leave this mystery to God and the English. The English usually feel the same way about American baseball."[29]

Having grown up playing cricket in South Africa, I've found again and again that trying to explain cricket to Americans is a well-nigh impossible task. The reason is simple. Try though they might, Americans cannot help comparing it with baseball. So they cannot grasp why you would have two batters in at the same time. Or why the batters run back and forth on the twenty-two-yard pitch rather than running round the bases. Nor does cricket's arcane terminology of "bowling a maiden over" or a field position known as "silly mid-on" help matters. To say nothing of the fact that an international match can last five days.

The difficulty for Americans is not merely the vocabulary; it's an inability to understand that cricket is a totally different game from baseball and it's futile to try to compare the two. Just like us trying to compare the Kingdom of God with our earthly kingdoms, a problem that even Jesus struggled to overcome after three years of teaching disciples. They couldn't understand He was trying to introduce them to a totally different contest from the one they thought they were playing.

Far from offering to take on the Romans and overthrow their hold on the children of Israel, Jesus' messianic message was of a totally different order. As Jesus said, "My Kingdom is not of this world. If it were, My servants would fight to prevent My arrest by the Jewish leaders. But now My Kingdom is from another place." (Jn. 18:36)

Despite all that Jesus had taught them, the disciples still didn't get what kind of Kingdom Jesus was introducing. Think for example of James

---

[29] Peter Kreeft: *Jacob's Ladder*.

40

and John and their unseemly ambition when they asked Jesus to put them on His right hand and left hand when He came to glory. He made it plain that they were asking the wrong question. (Mk. 10:35-40) It was only after the resurrection that they and the other disciples realized they'd been playing by the rules of the wrong game.

In stark contrast to James and John seeking to advance their own interests, Jesus calls His disciples to shuck off our secular world's priorities of success, wealth, and power, and instead to be servants of all and to take up their crosses and follow Him. It is as if the Son of God has called a pick-up game and points to us one by one, inviting us to join His team for a game that we cannot lose.

41

26: Crisis Readiness

Be always on the watch, and pray that you may be able to escape all that is about to happen....

– Luke 21:36

Eric Moody was the pilot of a Boeing 747, on a British Airways flight from Kuala Lampur, capital of Malaysia, to Perth, Australia, on June 24, 1982.[30] With typical British understatement, he made the following announcement to his passengers: "Good evening ladies and gentlemen. This is your captain speaking. We have a small problem. All four engines have stopped. We are doing our damnedest to get them going again. I trust you are not in too much distress."

Well, if they weren't before, they surely had good reason to be now. The problem was that the plane had encountered ash from an unexpected eruption from the volcano Galunggun on Java. Moody was able to restart the plane and landed it safely even though the windshield was almost completely opaque because of damage from the ash.

Moody didn't begin his "crisis day" with the slightest expectation of what lay ahead. Nor can any of us know what crisis may lie ahead—today, tomorrow, next month. But Moody's thousands of hours of flying time and intensive simulator training for various emergencies enabled him to keep his cool and stay focused on managing his crisis.[31]

So too with us, if we are able to fall back on a firmly grounded faith. No, we don't need to log the equivalent of thousands of hours of "crisis preparation." God is more concerned with the depth than the duration of our walk with Him. The question is, therefore, how strong a foundation would be in place if a crisis were thrust upon us today, tomorrow, or next month? If we need a reminder of our capacity to cope with whatever life might bring our way, we need only consider the hymn, "How Firm a

---

[30] https://en.wikipedia.org/wiki/British_Airways_Flight_009. Accessed Sept. 4, 2023.

[31] For an equally dramatic story of a plane landing safely against all the odds, you may want to read about the "Miracle on the Hudson." That's when Capt. Chesley Sullenberger glided flight US 1549 to landing on New York's Hudson River on January 15, 2009, following a bird strike that killed all the plane's engines. A National Transportation Safety Board official called it "the most successful ditching in aviation history."

Foundation."[32] Here are the first four verses:

> *How firm a foundation, ye saints of the Lord,*
> *Is laid for your faith in His excellent word!*
> *What more can He say than to you He hath said,*
> *To you who for refuge to Jesus have fled?*

> *Fear not, I am with thee, O be not dismayed,*
> *For I am thy God, and will still give thee aid;*
> *I'll strengthen thee, help thee, and cause thee to stand,*
> *Upheld by My righteous, omnipotent hand.*

> *When through the deep waters I call thee to go,*
> *The rivers of sorrow shall not overflow;*
> *For I will be with thee, thy troubles to bless,*
> *And sanctify to thee thy deepest distress.*

> *When through fiery trials thy pathway shall lie,*
> *My grace all sufficient, shall be thy supply;*
> *The flame shall not hurt thee; I only design*
> *Thy dross to consume, and thy gold to refine.*

---

[32] The hymn's authorship is unclear. It has been attributed both to a certain George Keith as well as someone named R. Keen.

27: The Dawn and Death

...our Savior, Christ Jesus, ... has destroyed death.

— 2 Timothy 1:10

~~~~~

Death for the Christian is turning off the light because the dawn has come.

— Leon Jaworski[33]

We use a range of euphemisms to describe death. In fact, it's fair to say that people in the increasingly secular West no longer die. They pass on. They rest in peace. They slip away or breathe their last. Christians, though, have a thoroughly realistic view of death. Our theology gives us no excuse to avoid talking about its brutal ugliness and cruelty. But that is only Part 1. Part 2 speaks of the victory over death that Jesus accomplished on the cross. As Paul writes of Jesus, he "has destroyed death and has brought life and immortality to light through the gospel." (2 Tim. 1:10)

With that reality in mind, then, how are Christians to speak of and understand the nature of death? One way is to reflect on Leon Jaworski's analogy of death being like switching out the light because a new day has come.

Whether it is the death of someone else, or as we approach our own, we cope with the darkness as best we can, with what lighting we can provide — and it gives us comfort. But then comes the dawn, a new day filled with God's brilliant sunlight. Now we can see everything, not only our immediate surroundings that our meagre and artificial light illuminated. Now, instead, our puny effort at lighting seems irrelevant.

As Paul predicted for his Corinthian readers in his celebrated chapter on love, "... we know in part and we prophesy in part, but when completeness comes, what is in part disappears.... For now we see only a reflection as in a mirror; then we shall see face to face. Now I know in part; then I shall know fully, even as I am fully known." (1 Cor. 13:9-12)

So too with death: what a difference daylight makes, now that dawn has come.

---

[33] Quoted in Gordon S. Jackson: *Quotes for the Journey, Wisdom for the Way.*

28: The Diverter

Brothers and sisters, if someone is caught in a sin, you who live by the Spirit should restore that person gently. But watch yourselves, or you also may be tempted.

— Galatians 6:1

The typical US bathtub and shower combination has a device that allows you switch the flow of water from the spout to the shower. Also typically, you'll start a shower by running the water through the spout. Then you turn to this thingy called a diverter, which you'll need to push, pull, lift, or do something else to get the water flowing from the shower head.

This action is so routine that when you're showering at home you may not notice a problem that can arise slowly over time. Especially if you have hard water coming through your pipes, a chemical buildup in the diverter valve will cause more and more water to come trickling through the spout, leaving you with less water fed through the shower head. This change will happen so slowly that you may not even notice it. But then one day you ask yourself, "How come so much water is coming through the spout?" And you realize it's time either to replace the diverter valve or try repairing it by cleaning off that chemical buildup.

The situation is not unlike the gradual slippage we can experience in our relationship with God. We find ourselves resembling the church in Laodicea, assailed for its lukewarmness, neither hot nor cold in its love. (Rev. 3:16) Like a married couple who slowly drift apart until one day they realize they no longer have anything in common, we and God may increasingly become distant. But it has rightly been said that if God seems far away, who do you think moved?

The Tempter doesn't care what could be causing this widening gap; he's quite content with even a slow drift away from God. He is patient as long as the trend continues. Like the slow drip of water on a stone or concrete, imperceptibly wearing it down over time, the changes in the "divine diverter" in our lives may similarly reflect a slowly diminishing commitment to God.

Time to invite God in for some plumbing work? The good news is that He is on call 24/7.

29: Don't Look

[I]f your eye causes you to stumble, gouge it out and throw it away. It is better for you to enter life with one eye than to have two eyes and be thrown into the fire of hell.

— *Matthew 18:9*

We begin with, of all people, a naked woman on horseback: Lady Godiva. This eleventh century Anglo-Saxon noblewoman was angered by her husband's increased taxation of the locals. He agreed to change his mind if she rode naked on horseback, covering herself only with her long hair, through the streets of Coventry — a story based in fact. What is less clear is the authenticity of the story about a local tailor known as Tom, who legend says violated Lady Godiva's demand that everyone stay indoors, with their shutters closed. Tom, according to Wikipedia's account of the legend, bore a hole in his shutters to take a look, and was struck blind. His legacy was to leave us the unsavory eponym of a Peeping Tom, and an unexpected starting point for our reflections. Regardless of the truth of this story, its moral was plain: "Look at what should not be seen, and you'll pay a price; play by the rules, and you'll be okay."

For Christians, there are two sets of things in everyday life "that should not be seen." The first concerns the norms of our society. Each culture has taboos on what we should not look at. In some cultures, making direct eye contact with someone of superior rank is a no-no. Likewise, a woman with uncovered breasts walking down Main Street in a U.S. city will soon get attention from law enforcement, in addition to others whose interest she has attracted. In many traditional African societies, however, she would fit in perfectly.

Like other tactful, caring and sensitive members of our society, Christians know what is expected of them regarding these taboos. But more is required of us. As the children's song has it, "Watch your eyes, watch your eyes, what they see." Some things that might be acceptable in our society are off limits to Christians seeking to live holy lives pleasing to God. While pornography is legal in most Western societies,[34] and widespread on the Internet, this is clearly a no-go zone for Christians. Similarly, some of the intrusive, demeaning, and dehumanizing content

---

[34] Child pornography is generally in a category of its own, and illegal in the United States and many other countries.

that sometimes characterizes reality TV programming is surely antithetical to the dignity God wants accorded to each of His creatures.

Christians, therefore, need to "watch their eyes" with particular care. In his book on icons, Henri Nouwen says that we are always seeing. "When we dream, we see. When we stare in front of us, we see. When we close our eyes to rest, we see. We see trees, houses, roads and cars, seas and mountains, animals and people, places and faces, shapes and colors. We see clearly or vaguely, but always we find something to see."[35] Then, importantly, he adds: "Just as we are responsible for what we eat, so we are responsible for what we see."

Scripture gives both general advice about "watching our eyes," as well as sobering object lessons. Jesus Himself says "[I]f your eye causes you to stumble, gouge it out and throw it away. It is better for you to enter life with one eye than to have two eyes and be thrown into the fire of hell." (Mt. 18:9) If you are troubled by visual temptation, Jesus is saying, then do not look. Like Eve, you could easily rationalize the next steps that will oh-so-smoothly lead you from seeing to sinning.

It is not only bad things we should avoid seeing. We can be exposed to only so much of God's holiness. Even Moses could not see God face to face. When he encounters the glory of the Lord, God tells him, "[Y]ou cannot see My face, for no one may see Me and live." (Ex. 33:20)[36] That is not the warning we typically need, however; our eyes are far more likely to lure us into sin than over-exposure to God's holiness.

And what about that which God sees? The writer of Hebrews says, "Nothing in all creation is hidden from God's sight. Everything is uncovered and laid bare before the eyes of Him to whom we must give account." (Heb. 4:13) For trying to hide things *from God* is the height of folly. But when it comes to our own seeing, we could do worse than pray the Sarum Missal, a prayer dating to the eleventh century, the same era as Lady Godiva, the one on whom Peeping Tom should not have looked:

> *God be in my head*
> *And in my understanding;*
> *God be in myne eyes,*
> *And in my looking….*

---

[35] Henri Nouwen, *Behold the Beauty of the Lord: Praying with Icons*.

[36] Earlier, in Exodus 24:9-11 we read how Moses, Aaron and other leaders "went up and saw the God of Israel. … [T]hey saw God, and they ate and drank." But the *NIV Study Bible's* notes on John 1:18 reconcile these passages: "[S]ince no human being can see God as he really is, those who saw God saw him in a form he took on himself temporarily for the occasion." *The NIV Study Bible*.

30: Dust in the Sunlight

... if we walk in the light, as he is in the light, we have fellowship with one another, and the blood of Jesus His Son cleanses us from all sin.

– 1 John 1:7, Revised Standard Version

You've done a thorough job of cleaning the house: dusting, vacuuming, polishing, scrubbing, disinfecting and whatever else you deemed necessary. After proclaiming victory, you sit back and sip a well-earned cup of tea.

Then you realize you've made the mistake of sitting in your favorite chair which, at this time of day, is catching the brilliant sunlight coming through the kitchen window that's now sparkling clean, and making disappointingly visible all that dust your efforts stirred up and is now taunting you as it floats in the air. No matter how rigorous your cleaning, it's obvious your work is far from perfect. Even if you returned to the cleaning, you concede that your efforts will never reach perfection.

So too with our sinfulness when exposed to the dazzling light of God's holiness. No matter how hard we've tried to get our act together, how diligently we've worked at doing good and avoiding harm, the house is still dirty by God's standards. It is God, and God alone, who can cleanse us from all sin. As John puts it, "... if we walk in the light, as he is in the light, we have fellowship with one another, and the blood of Jesus his Son cleanses us from all sin." (1 Jn. 1:7, *Revised Standard Version*)

31: The Embassy

For he will command his angels concerning you to guard you in all your ways.

— Psalm 91:11

I have led six student groups on month-long trips to South Africa, where I grew up. Toward the end of our stay, we would visit the US embassy in Pretoria, a fortress-like, foreboding place built toward the end of the apartheid era, when nobody could predict how peacefully that country would transition from white domination to black majority rule. So the architects fashioned a building that, in the post 9-11 period, now affords the embassy and its staff an extraordinary degree of safety.

After our students have shown their IDs and gone through the two security screenings, including leaving behind their cameras, they get a sudden assurance of safety on getting into the building itself. There is a sense, especially after walking past the Marine guards, that virtually nothing can touch you here. You certainly feel protected from whatever threats you might face outside this building, located as it is in a country notorious for its crime rate. For now, at least, you feel safe. And in any embassy, that is exactly how it is supposed to be.

The great missionary David Livingstone said, "I am immortal until the will of God for me is accomplished."[37] We are in God's hands, and nothing—absolutely nothing—can harm us without His knowledge and consent. As Christians, we can know we operate with a unique, divine kind of immunity; no person, force, or circumstances can thwart God's will for us as we live out our calling to be His ambassadors.

No, we don't work or live in Christian fortresses. And physically, Christians are as prone to whatever threats or dangers face the rest of society. We can look to the psalms and other parts of Scripture, however, for one assurance after the other that God is looking after us. Psalm 18 says, "The Lord is my rock, my fortress and my deliverer; my God is my rock, in Whom I take refuge." (Ps. 18:2) Elsewhere the psalmist asks, "where does my help come from?" (Ps. 12:1) No, not the hills, but from the Lord Himself. Five times in this psalm of eight verses, the psalmist reminds himself how God "watches over" us. Throughout the rest of the Old Testament and the New, we hear echoes of this theme: The God Who is aware when even a sparrow dies, urges us to put our trust in Him. "So

---

[37] Quoted in Gordon S. Jackson: *Quotes for the Journey, Wisdom for the Way.*

don't be afraid," Jesus said. "You are worth more than many sparrows." (Mt. 10:31)

As Christ's ambassadors to His world, we know we may at times be placed in harm's way because of our faith. We need look only to Paul's beatings, imprisonments, and deprivations to know that sometimes living out our faith may carry a physical price. Or we look at the martyrdom of Stephen and realize God may ask of us even our lives in serving Him.

When countries exchange ambassadors, they do so on the clear understanding that because these are individuals with special status, the receiving country has a strong obligation to protect all foreign ambassadors, their embassies and consulates, and the personnel attached to them. Similarly, we serve a God Who is both able and willing to protect His children. Even though, like Job, we are at times subjected to the worst the world throws our way, it is never without God's knowledge and permission. In Him alone, then, is our safety and security, at a level that infinitely surpasses even that of the US embassy in Pretoria.

32: The Entrance Fee

The Kingdom of Heaven is like treasure hidden in a field. When a man found it, he hid it again, and then in his joy went and sold all he had and bought that field.

– Matthew 13:44

The option for a brief getaway looked promising. The condo unit would give us easy access to the sightseeing we wanted to do nearby, as well as allow us to self-cater when not splurging on a meal out. And the price was reasonable too.

Then we read the small print. We expected the local sales tax (in this case 8 percent). But then there was the 9 percent destination fee, a 6 percent tourism fee, and a vaguely described "property service" fee of 18 percent. In total, these slapped another 41 percent on what had once seemed like a reasonable cost. But wait, as they used to say in those ads for a nuclear-powered potato peeler for only $9.99, there's more: the cleaning fee. In this case, $96. So, if you'll tolerate two more numbers (thank you), this means that for a rental of $100, we'd end up paying $238 for a one-night visit.[38] All we could say was, "Are you kidding?"

Hidden or unexpected fees rank high among things that irritate Americans most. A 2021 survey reported that 40 percent of Americans ranked hidden charges as their biggest financial pet peeve, ahead even of steep bank charges and having to file one's taxes.

Why? People hate the feeling of being deceived, drawn into buying a certain item or service, only to be unpleasantly surprised by one charge after another. Like a "resort fee" at a hotel or being charged for a room safe that you didn't use or want. Or a restaurant that decides in advance that you will pay a 20 percent tip, regardless of the service you receive.

By contrast, when you turn to God, you'll find no hidden charges. God, like the prodigal son's father, seeks nothing of us except that we "return home." God awaits us with open arms, running toward us as we shame-facedly repent of having turned our backs on our heavenly Father. There is nothing for us to do except accept God's love and forgiveness, knowing that we are the beneficiary of sheer, unmerited grace. As someone said, "We cannot earn by our merit what Christ has secured for

---

[38] These figures are based on an actual, but soon aborted, quest for a weekend getaway.

us by His grace." In other words, there are no "hidden charges" required of us once we as prodigal children return home. Whatever price had to be paid has been taken care of on the cross.

But then there's the paradox. As Henry Drummond put it, "The entrance fee to the Kingdom of Heaven is nothing, the annual subscription is everything."[39] God does not want a half-hearted commitment from us. On the contrary, as Paul says, we are to present ourselves as a living sacrifice to God. (Rom. 12:1) We are, he continues, not to conform to this world's standards. Jesus Himself tells us the parable of the man who finds treasure hidden in a field and sells all he has to acquire it (Mt. 13:44), "it" being the Kingdom of God.

So there we have it: No hidden fees on entering God's Kingdom, now or later. But we're expected to sign over everything to Him, giving all we have to acquire that treasure of immeasurable value.

---

[39] Quoted in Gordon S. Jackson: *Quotes for the Journey, Wisdom for the Way.*

33: Entropy Versus Negentropy

Therefore let us move beyond the elementary teachings about Christ and be taken forward to maturity...

— Hebrews 6:1

Let's begin with "entropy," one definition of which is a "gradual decline into disorder." The idea is that over the long term, everything in a system wears down, breaks, or collapses. Our sun, for example, will one day burn out. Our bodies wear out. No computer lasts forever.

Negentropy is the opposite. It means things are becoming more organized or structured, or heading toward wholeness.

And negentropy marks the healthy Christian life. The writer of Hebrews urges his readers, **"Therefore let us move beyond the elementary teachings about Christ and be taken forward to maturity...."** (Heb. 6:1) Unlike the sun, ourselves, or our computers, we're heading in the opposite direction: toward an uncorruptible wholeness, or as the *King James Version's* wording of this verse urges us, "...let us go on unto perfection." During our earthly lives we are to grow in maturity in our faith. Paul tells his Philippian readers to **"continue to work out your salvation with fear and trembling...."** (Phil. 2:12) **We have much yet to do, this side of eternity, to live out our faith.** But it is only in heaven that our "negentropic journey" will culminate, as we see the fulfillment of God's promise when He will "...present you before His glorious presence without fault and with great joy." (Jd. 24) **In other words, no more entropy.**

34: Essential Workers

Then he said to his disciples, "The harvest is plentiful but the workers are few."

— Matthew 9:37

The COVID-19 pandemic taught us all kinds of lessons, among them the nature of "essential workers." Who exactly fit this description varied from state to state. Everywhere, health workers, grocery store employees, and regular emergency staff were designated as essential. (Oddly, the governor of Florida, Ron DeSantis, deemed that World Wrestling Entertainment could continue offering bouts because the company was an "essential business.")

By contrast, God has always regarded every one of the citizens of his Kingdom as essential workers. We're all indispensable in His service.

A legend underscores this point. Upon Jesus' ascension to heaven, the angels welcomed Him and asked, "What are Your plans now, Lord?"

Jesus replied, "I've entrusted My team of disciples to spread the gospel message throughout the world."

"But what if that doesn't work?" the angels asked. "What is Your Plan B?"

"I have no Plan B," Jesus said.

Just as those eleven surviving disciples[40] were essential workers, so too are the rest of us. Jesus has no Plan B.

---

[40] Later supplemented by the appointment of Matthias to join their ranks.

35: Experts in Goodness

I want you to be expert in goodness....
— *Romans 16:19*, Revised English Bible

Writer Malcolm Gladwell's 2008 book, *Outliers*, made the case that people who rose to the top of their fields did so because of the "10,000-hour rule." This was the idea that people like Bill Gates and the Beatles had put in enormous amounts of "practice" in their sphere of activity. The book soared to the top of bestseller lists. It popularized the notion that success took long hours of commitment.

This premise drew criticism as being over-simplistic. One needed certain innate skills or a good genetic legacy to become an NBA basketball player; if you were physically ill-equipped, no matter how much you practiced you could never make it to the top.

Still, regardless of the validity of Gladwell's thesis, which could be paraphrased as that old adage, "Practice makes perfect," there's a powerful lesson here for Christians. Paul, writing to the Romans, urges them to become "expert in goodness." That's how the *Revised English Bible* translates it, using wording similar to that of the J. B. Phillips version. Most other translations speak of needing to become "wise in what is good" or variations on that theme.

The message is clear: Christians need to become specialists (for that's what an expert is), in goodness and wisdom. How do we get there? The same way as the punchline in that old joke about a visitor to New York asking how to get to Carnegie Hall, and the local responds, "Practice, man; practice."

So too with us. Like the beginning pianist or teacher or soccer player, or whatever sphere you choose, you need hours and hours of hard work at your craft before you can attain expert status. The goal, as Jesus told His disciples, is that we are to "Be perfect ... as your heavenly Father is perfect." (Mt. 5:48)

36: The Failing Body — A Pastor's Prayer

The body is a unit, though it is made up of many parts; and though all its parts are many, they form one body. So it is with Christ.

— 1 Corinthians 12:12

Lord, Woody Allen said, "My main regret in life is that I'm not someone else."

Well, I don't know about him, but could You make my church someone else?

Lord, my church is in trouble.
We're just limping along.
We should be a church that runs and jumps.
Instead, we hobble and stumble.

We struggle merely to stand up straight;
When we do, it seems we hurt everywhere else.
We need knee replacement surgery.
And a couple of new hips.

Lord, You know how much old Mrs. Dodds annoys everyone:
With her whining, her sullen ingratitude, her perpetual snippiness.
I don't know if she's a hip or a knee or some other part of Your body,
But if anyone is a candidate for a transplant, Lord, she is.

Her attitude contaminates us all, it seems.
So many in the church have a sour disposition.
We're not dealing with our body's toxicity as we should.
Would a kidney or liver transplant help?

And judging from the fights at our church council meetings,
I think we need a heart transplant too.
Or at least a few valve replacements.

Ours is a church that's so inward looking, Lord;
We see nothing beyond ourselves.
I fear we need a pair of cornea transplants.

The few visitors we get can see that our face no longer shows the beauty You gave us.

It is scarred from our fighting, our negativity, our nursing of grudges.
I know this is still pioneering medical technology, Lord,
But might You be able to arrange one of those face transplants?

Lord, this is far from a healthy body I'm trying to lead.
I think we may have we reached that point:
This body of believers needs a full-body transplant.

We need to be someone else.

But if that's too much to ask for,
Could You meanwhile at least give us
Some healthy, fully functional new body parts?
Please.

But if You can't do that either,
Could You at least create a new heart in me?

~~~~~

Is there anything in this satire that strikes a chord with you? If so, what is it?

37: Fighting in the Lifeboats

Don't have anything to do with foolish and stupid arguments, because you know they produce quarrels. And the Lord's servant must not be quarrelsome but must be kind to everyone, able to teach, not resentful.

— 2 Timothy 2:23-24

The gospel message, reduced to its simplest, is that Jesus came to save us from our sins. As Karl Barth said, "We must read the Bible through the eyes of shipwrecked people for whom everything has gone overboard." The shipwreck has forced us to abandon ship and take to the God-provided lifeboats that alone are our salvation.

Two astonishing things are worth noting. One is the sheer grace of a God Who sends us lifeboats when we ourselves have steered our ship onto the rocks. The other is how some of us conduct ourselves in those lifeboats. We start to fight. Having been miraculously saved from drowning, we begin to squabble. It may be a minor issue. As we bob along in the water, your knee keeps jabbing my thigh; I ask if you could move slightly to your left. You happily agree, cramped though we are. And all is well.

Or it may be more irritating: Your four-year-old keeps singing "Old MacDonald had a Farm," off-key, time after time. Like everyone else in the boat, I am soaking wet and cold. And have a Level 4 headache. I ask you more snippily than is warranted to get him to stop. You reply with equal snippiness and several of our fellow passengers join in, taking either your side or mine. Before long, we have a full-fledged shouting match under way.

Or let's say fighting breaks out over water rations. One of the elderly passengers is clearly gravely ill, to the point that a nurse who is in our boat quietly says the woman is at death's door. Some passengers begin arguing that we should divide up her water ration among the rest of us, as she's likely to die soon. Others object. The ensuing argument leads to a fistfight between the ill woman's son and two of the other men. Other passengers leap up, trying to stop them, and in the ensuing ruckus the boat begins to rock dangerously from side to side, threatening everyone's survival.

~~~~~

By now you get the point. These lifeboats, our local churches, are where we are to live out our miraculous, God-provided rescue. As in lifeboats, we are to put up with sometimes irritating people, limited resources, clashes over values and beliefs, or other conflicts. At times, perhaps following deep and sincerely held doctrinal differences, a split in a church may be the best outcome for all. But in Protestant churches in particular, Christians are often too ready to jump from one lifeboat to another or try to force some of their fellow-passengers to do so. And what might be the sources of these voluntary or forced acts of "jumping ship"?

The pastor never once visited me in the hospital after my surgery.

I think that spending $12,500 on a new sound system is unconscionable.

The pastor's sermons about God's demands for justice were blatantly political.

The new music director gives us nothing but fluff.

[Fill in a reason of your own: ....]

So it is that God must look upon His rescued people with a mix of grief and anger at how soon these people in the lifeboats forget the grace that has saved them—and how close some of these boats are to capsizing.

38: Fleeting Francium

A thousand years in your sight are like a day that has just gone by, or like a watch in the night.

— *Psalm 90:4*

Eric Weiner notes in his book *The Geography of Bliss* that, "Of all the substances known to man, the least stable is something called francium. It's never lasted longer than 22 minutes. At any given time there is only one ounce of francium in the earth's crust. 'Vanishingly rare' is how it's often described."

Fortunately, we humans are afforded a longer lifespan than that. The Bible says: "Our days may come to seventy years, or eighty, if our strength endures; yet the best of them are but trouble and sorrow, for they quickly pass, and we fly away." (Ps. 90:10)

Yet to put our average lifespans in context, it's helpful to look at two other numbers. Scientists have calculated that universe is 14 billion years old and that our planet is 4.54 billion years old (with an error range of 50 million years).[41] For those of us who can't think beyond next Wednesday, trying to grasp 50 million years, let alone a billion, is impossible.

Given the brevity of our time on earth, then, it may be tempting to see our lives and our contributions as pointless, in the great scheme of things. Until we consider the reminder of the English missionary, C.T. Studd. He wrote in a poem: "Only one life, 'twill soon be past. Only what's done for Christ will last."[42] Christians are assured throughout Scripture that human life is of infinite value and that, short though they are, our lives are an integral part of God's overall plan. As the *New Zealand Prayer Book* has it, "[W]ith you nothing is wasted or incomplete."

---

[41] *https://www.space.com/24854-how-old-is-earth.html*. Accessed Sept. 4, 2023.
[42] Numerous citations on the Internet. Original source unknown.

39: Flotsam and Jetsam

I consider everything a loss because of the surpassing worth of knowing Christ Jesus my Lord, for whose sake I have lost all things. I consider them garbage, that I may gain Christ.

— Philippians 3:8

For anyone who sails the seas, flotsam and jetsam are unhappy, unwelcome words. Flotsam is wreckage or debris that's floating after things have gone badly wrong; either your vessel was hit by heavy weather, leading to a loss of equipment that was washed overboard, or worse still, these are the remnants of your ship going down.

Jetsam, by contrast, is whatever you've chosen to throw overboard in a desperate bid to save your vessel in dire conditions. We read in Acts 27, for example, of Paul's experience as his ship bound for Rome encountered serious trouble: "We took such a violent battering from the storm that the next day they began to throw the cargo overboard. On the third day, they threw the ship's tackle overboard with their own hands." (Acts 27:18-19)

This echoes the experience we read about in Jonah, where the sailors toss their cargo overboard in an attempt to lighten the ship in the middle of a fearful storm — before they jettison Jonah as well. (Jo 1:5 and 1:15)

What about us, who are on dry land, going about our business? Now and again, it may be that we encounter one of those storms of life. It could be a critically ill child. Dismissal from a job. Getting caught up in a scandal that ruins your reputation and credibility. Whatever it is, it's at those times you are most likely to realize afresh (or perhaps only for the first time) what is truly important. As a result, you are ready, metaphorically speaking, to toss overboard everything that's non-essential in your life. You will do anything to save your four-year-old. That may mean wiping out your savings or saying "no" to that dream job in Cleveland. The result is you now see once-precious cargo floating in the water around you, as the storm rages. Your prayers for calm seem to go unanswered, except for hearing God say, "Toss even more over the side. Get rid of the non-essentials if you want to keep this ship afloat." And out of obedience, you do.

Eventually, the storm ends. It has cost you your cargo but you saved the ship, your crew, and your passengers. As you continue your journey in what are now calm waters you notice something bobbing in the water a hundred yards off the port bow: the flotsam from another vessel, one that didn't survive the storm, including cargo that could have, should have, been discarded. You alert your crew to look for possible survivors.

Then you write up the events in the ship's log, adding this reflection: "What does it profit a captain if he cares more for his cargo than for life itself?"

40: Flying Fish and Numinous Moments

Jesus took Peter, James and John with him and led them up a high mountain, where they were all alone. There he was transfigured before them.

— Mark 9:2

"Numinous": Defined by Merriam-Webster's online dictionary as "filled with a sense of the presence of divinity."

So called "flying fish" are fascinating creatures. They can leap out of the water and, relying on specially evolved wing-like fins, can glide for up to forty-five seconds on the water's surface. Typically, they fly for about 160 feet, although fish catching an updraft of air have been recorded flying as far as 1,400 feet.

So, why do they do this and why do they have a place in a book of devotional readings? First, marine biologists think the behavior is an attempt to escape predators. But it's a parallel to our spiritual lives that merits their attention in our thinking. Like the fish, we normally live in a certain realm. They are creatures of the sea; we are earthly beings. But also like the fish, we are designed to escape or transcend that environment at times. We may experience these moments in worship, in prayer, or in some kind of mystical encounter with God. These moments of transcending the ordinary allow us, however briefly, to experience God's presence. In other words, we're talking about numinous moments, like numerous instances described in the Bible. Examples include Jesus' transfiguration, Moses' encounter with the burning bush, and the intrusions of angels into people's lives that change them forever. These experiences are all fleeting, however. We humans cannot live in the rarefied numinous atmosphere for long. Instead, fueled by those encounters, we return to our normal habitat, where we live out the bulk of our lives.

Not everyone accepts that numinous encounters are possible. In our secular age, these individuals would be like skeptical flying fish who don't believe it's possible to leave their watery home, even for a moment or two; they dismiss all this business of "flying" and "air" as nonsense. Most flying fish know better and live out their existence knowing that, for at least part of the time, they're made for another arena. And so are we.

63

41: Four Out of Five

If any of you lacks wisdom, you should ask God, Who gives generously to all without finding fault, and it will be given to you. But when you ask, you must believe and not doubt, because the one who doubts is like a wave of the sea, blown and tossed by the wind.

– James 1:5-6

Imagine you're on the way to the airport for a vacation abroad. You do a last-minute mental inventory.

1. Travel insurance? Check.
2. Boarding pass and ticket info? Check.
3. Credit cards? Check.
4. Luggage, including your meds? Check.
5. Passport?

Passport? Oops. You now realize that it's still sitting in your safety deposit box at your bank. You're unlikely to keep going and say, "Well, four out of five isn't bad. It'll be okay."

There's a similar five-step checklist Christians ought to apply to any major decisions they face. Each of these steps should receive a positive response before moving ahead. They are:

1. Is the decision I'm considering compatible with Scriptural guidelines?
2. Have I committed this decision to extended and earnest prayer?
3. Have I sought the advice of mature Christians on the wisdom of this decision?
4. How does this decision fit the circumstances I am facing? and
5. Do I have a sense of inner peace about my decision?

Until you've got a "thumbs up" on each of the five, you're probably not ready to make a decision. If, for example, you're seriously thinking of leaving your job to go to seminary, and your closest friends are advising you against it, you need to check your thinking. Or if you've been invited to go on a short-term mission trip, and the first four points check out just fine, yet you've still got a nagging feeling that something isn't right, once again it may be best to hold off your decision.

Is it possible that your friends' advice is wrong? Or that you're confusing a lack of inner peace about a decision with plain old nervousness? Of course. The point isn't that missing one of these five checkpoints means you shouldn't go ahead; it simply means there's a warning light on the dashboard and you're well advised to take a second look at what's happening. Or, to switch metaphors, if these five principles don't line up neatly like lights on a runway, you need to question seriously whether you're ready to come in for a landing.

C.S. Lewis addresses the complexity of how the various dimensions of guidance work together. "I don't doubt that the Holy Spirit guides your decisions from within when you make them with the intention of pleasing God. The error would be to think that He speaks *only* within, whereas in reality He speaks also through Scripture, the church, Christian friends, books, etc."[43]

The lesson? We need to take a holistic approach to guidance, ensuring that all the pieces fit together. Omitting even one of these five steps can present a significant bump in the road of your Christian journey. Just like leaving your passport behind.

---

[43] C. S. Lewis: *The Collected Letters Vol III.*

42: Giants and the Wilderness

Dear friends, do not be surprised at the fiery ordeal that has come on you to test you, as though something strange were happening to you.

— 1 Peter 4:12

So, what did you expect: that Christianity would be a problem-free ride? That it would all be plain sailing? Or to use yet another cliché, no bumps in the road? Of course, you should have expected problems along the way, perhaps as you tried to figure out your role on a secular college campus or in a secular office environment. Or maybe you've encountered surprising hostility or opposition from people you expected would be supportive. No matter the source, you're dealing with exactly the kinds of trials the apostle Peter discusses in his first epistle, chapter 4. As he puts it, "Dear friends, do not be surprised at the fiery ordeal that has come on you to test you, as though something strange were happening to you." (1 Pet. 4:12)

This is normal for the Christian life, as it was for the children of Israel en route to the Promised Land. Joshua and Caleb were among the twelve spies sent to check out the land and came back with a favorable report. But their recommendation to move ahead was overridden by the others, as we read in Numbers:

> But the men that went up with him said, We be not able to go up against the people; for they are stronger than we. And they brought up an evil report of the land which they had searched unto the children of Israel, saying, The land, through which we have gone to search it, is a land that eateth up the inhabitants thereof; and all the people that we saw in it are men of a great stature. And there we saw the giants, the sons of Anak, which come of the giants: and we were in our own sight as grasshoppers, and so we were in their sight. (Num. 13:31-33, King James Version)

The sons of Anak, the giants, were seen as too much a threat. And so the Israelites were condemned to wandering the desert for forty years more because of the reluctance of these ten men to trust in Yahweh, who had not only brought them to the brink of the Promised Land, but was ready to lead them to finish the journey.

As the devotional anthology, *Streams in the Desert*, puts it, "It is when we are in the way of duty that we find giants. It was when Israel was going forward that the giants appeared. When they turned back into the wilderness they found none."

So what giants are you facing today? Are you ready, with the help of the God Who has led you thus far, to move forward and face them head on? Or will you turn back, into a wilderness of your own, where you will find none?

43: Giving God Pitocin

Do not be anxious about anything, but in every situation, by prayer and petition, with thanksgiving, present your requests to God.

— Philippians 4:6

If you're an expectant mom and your baby's showing no signs of joining the human race any time soon, your doctor or midwife may well introduce you to Pitocin. It's the brand name of a synthetic hormone that mirrors the natural one you have in your body, oxytocin. Both serve to trigger contractions. So if you're one or two weeks overdue, or if you have a medical condition like high blood pressure or diabetes, or if there are concerns about the baby's wellbeing, you may be given Pitocin through your IV, in slowly increasing doses to get labor going.

Millions of women have benefited from the synthetic form, almost all of them no doubt unaware of the meaning of the natural hormone: oxytocin, not to be confused with oxycontin, the highly addictive pain killer. Oxytocin is made up of two Greek words meaning "quick birth." And a quick and healthy birth is what we wish for all expectant moms.

But many of us must have wished there were some kind of divine version of Pitocin, that we could give God to hurry things along. When we read in Revelation that He promises to "make all things new," (Rev. 21:5, *King James Version*) we often find ourselves saying, "But *when?*"

Time to heed the advice of Stephen Merritt, who warned: "Cease meddling with God's plans and will. You touch anything of His and you mar the work. You may move the hands of a clock, but you do not change the time; so you may hurry the unfolding of God's will, but you harm and may not help the work."[44]

The apostle Peter points to the gap between our handle on time and that of the One who transcends time as we know it: "With the Lord a day is like a thousand years, and a thousand years are like a day." (2 Pet. 3:8) In ways we cannot conceive, He is able, and willing, to endure an unimaginably long labor to bring those "new things" into being, to match His perfect timing. And He does so without our offer of Pitocin, thank you very much.

It's been said that God is never in a hurry, but He's never late.

---

[44] https://www.dailychristianquote.com/stephen-merritt/. Accessed Sept. 4, 2023.

44: God's Indirect Speech Acts

For God does speak – now one way, now another – though no one perceives it.

– Job 33:14

~~~~~

It is always exceedingly difficult to get a direct answer from God.
– The Interpreter's Bible Commentary, on Job's question about his suffering

My communication studies colleagues at the university where I taught referred to a concept called an "indirect speech act." It entailed asking for something or saying something in a roundabout way, possibly out of politeness or to soften a request. For example, you may say, "Oh, it's hot in here." Your goal is to get your host to open the door or window, but you don't want to be so blunt as to say, "Open the door or window." Even with a "please" it still sounds bossy. Or you may ask, "Do you have the time?" when you're actually asking, "Please tell me the time." Or yet again, a friend says, "Would you like to get a cup of coffee?" and you respond, "I've got to study." You have not answered the person's question but been more polite, by softening the rejection with your indirect response. "No," or even "No, thanks," sounds harsher.

There are other reasons for giving people an indirect response, as we see in Scripture. Job, as we all know, had a tough time of it, unimaginably awful. Throughout that magnificent Old Testament book, we sympathize with this righteous man, asking along with him, "Why, O Lord," do You let him suffer such undeserved hardships?

Then, in chapters 38, 39 and the beginning of chapter 40, we get God's answer. Or, more correctly, God's non-answer. Instead, God answers a different question: "Do you have any idea who you're dealing with here?" In soaring poetry, God begins His reply:

Where were you when I laid the earth's foundation?
Tell Me, if you understand.
Who marked off its dimensions? Surely you know!
Who stretched a measuring line across it?
On what were its footings set,
 or who laid its cornerstone –
while the morning stars sang together
and all the angels shouted for joy? (Job 38:4-7)

Note too the sarcasm in the words, "Surely you know..." Of course Job doesn't know, as God takes this beleaguered man to task. Job has suffered greatly under God's permissive will, and then his pain is compounded by his friends, who presume to think they have the answers for his plight. At last God comes and blasts the friends' and Job's lack of understanding. But God doesn't answer their questions.

Nor does Jesus, when presented with the question, "Is it right to pay the imperial tax to Caesar or not?" (Mk. 12:14) Here too He doesn't answer directly but calls instead for a coin issued by the Roman rulers and confounds His questioners with His response.

Then, when the Pharisees ask Jesus by what authority He teaches, He replied, "I will also ask you one question. If you answer me, I will tell you by what authority I am doing these things. John's baptism — where did it come from? Was it from heaven, or of human origin?" (Mt. 21:24-25) Again, an indirect answer (or "non-answer") proves to be far more powerful than if He had answered their question directly.

What of our own lives? We need to watch for the motivation behind God's answers and non-answers to our prayers. If it seems God is responding with an indirect answer, let's look a little closer. For example:

"Lord, should I take that job in Orlando?"

And the Lord replies, "Have you thought about going to seminary?"

"Lord, you haven't answered my question?"

And the Lord says, "And you haven't answered Mine."

Why does God on occasion speak to us only indirectly? As we saw with Job and the answers Jesus gave to those trying to catch Him out, divine indirect speech acts may have much more to teach us than appear at first.

45: God's Privacy Policy

You have set our iniquities before you, our secret sins in the light of your presence.

– Psalm 90:8

Do you ever bother to read those written or emailed statements from our banks, medical providers, or others that outline their privacy policies? No, me neither. These organizations are legally required to keep us informed on how they gather information about us, what they do with it, who they can release it to (if anyone), and so on. We too establish our own privacy rules, at least when it comes to healthcare. We sign forms designating who can receive information about our medical condition, for example.

Given the massive data breaches that have occurred in recent years, people have good reason to fear that their personal data has been acquired by people with less than noble motivations. So, yes, privacy and its enforcement are a big deal.

But what if you got a statement in the mail tomorrow, directly from God, spelling out heaven's privacy policy? What might it say? And would you find it reassuring or deeply troubling? The document would probably say familiar things about not giving information about you to others without your permission. Basically, God will not snitch on you about the stationery you stole from the office last week. Nor, more seriously, need you fear that He'll tell your wife about that fling you had with a work colleague when you and she were away on that business trip.

The troubling part, though – and it really is troubling – is how much data God has in your file. It's everything. Not only your words and deeds, but even your thoughts. So that fantasizing you had about that colleague on the business trip, even though you didn't yield to temptation, or the anger that bubbled forth when that driver cut you off in traffic this morning and how you imagined doing him grievous bodily harm and savored immense pleasure at that prospect... Yes, it's all recorded. For unlike the Bank of America or your doctor, God knows "the secrets of the heart." (Ps. 44:21)

Paragraph twelve of God's privacy statement says, "Don't bother trying to hide stuff from Me. I see it all. I know all. Remember when you were a child and it seemed your mom had eyes in the back of her head, and seemed to see everything?" (The statement's far more informal than you expected.) "That's small potatoes compared with Me."

After asserting God's omniscience and omnipresence, the statement goes on to assure you that He's not interested in playing "gotcha games" with you. Instead, He wants you to live a life pleasing to Him — and that's in all areas of your life: thought, word and deed. This applies especially to those thoughts that nobody else will know, as well as words and deeds hidden from public view, words said in private, perhaps, that you'd be ashamed for others to hear, or deeds you now regret and hope are not discovered.

Then, paragraph fifteen speaks of repentance and forgiveness, quoting Psalm 103: "For as high as the heavens are above the earth, so great is his love for those who fear him; as far as the east is from the west, so far has he removed our transgressions from us." (Ps. 103:11-12)

As you have done so many times before, you confess your sins and ask God's forgiveness. You reflect on the infinite distance that lies between east and west. Now, all too aware of God's knowledge of the most private aspects of your life, you find yourself not threatened by God's privacy statement, but confident to affirm yet another verse from the psalms: "Test me, Lord, and try me, examine my heart and my mind..." (Ps. 26:2)

46: God's Temp Agency

During the night Paul had a vision of a man of Macedonia standing and begging him, "Come over to Macedonia and help us." After Paul had seen the vision, we got ready at once to leave for Macedonia, concluding that God had called us to preach the gospel to them.

— Acts 16:9-10

Whether you realize it or not, if you're a Christian, you're not only written in the "book of life" mentioned six times in Revelation, you're also listed with God's Temp Agency. He has you signed up for a particular task, or combination of tasks, right now. That could change at a moment's notice, however, as we see in the example of God summoning Paul to Macedonia.

A "temp" is exactly that: someone who is assigned for the time being to a particular job. The place where you're assigned may need you only until Friday; your agency will line up something else for next week. Sometimes you may have a longer-term posting somewhere, that runs to months or years. Yet no matter where you've been assigned, you work for the agency and it writes your paycheck.

So it is with us. We may be thrilled with our current assignment and, like many temp employees in real life, hope we can get a permanent position where we are. On the other hand, we may not particularly like our current assignment, yet we know we're there because the agency knows we're a good match for the task. We know too that we're working for God and it is to Him we look for our ultimate rewards.

How happy are you with your current God-given assignment? Is it time you wish God would move you elsewhere, or change your working conditions? Tell Him.

47: God's TSA

Let us then approach God's throne of grace with confidence, so that we may receive mercy and find grace to help us in our time of need.

— Hebrews 4:16

Yes, yes — we know all of us have immediate access to God in prayer, and that we can "boldly approach His throne of grace," (Heb. 4:16) just as we are with all our faults. Still, I have this fantasy that if I want to enter His presence, I first need to get past His TSA checkpoint.

I picture approaching the checkpoint staffed by uniformed angels, all cheerfully telling those of us in line what we can't carry any further. "No pride, please; be sure to leave all your pride in the discard bins. And no hypocrisy. Can't take that in either. Anger, lust, fear — all of it must go.

"No doubts either please. All in the bins, please." (They're super-polite, these angels.)

The person ahead of me goes through a scanner, which beeps an astonishingly beautiful few notes. An angel looks at him, with apparent amusement, and says, "Ah, still a touch of bigotry, I see. Toss it in the bin." The person sheepishly does so. The angel pats him on the back. "Okay, you're set to go," and he moves on.

Next, I approach the scanner, wondering if it'll pick up anything. I'm not fearful; I threw fear in the pre-scanner bin. But what else might it detect?

48: Grace: A Second Helping at the King's Banquet

Then he said to his servants, "The wedding banquet is ready, but those I invited did not deserve to come. So go to the street corners and invite to the banquet anyone you find."

— Matthew 22:8-9

The best things about a good buffet are the range of choices and your ability to make a second trip to the dessert section. Without succumbing to the sin of gluttony (we hope), you can eat to your heart's, or stomach's, content.

Imagine, though, having been invited to the banquet described in Matthew 22. The king hosts a wedding banquet for his son, Jesus tells us in this parable. But those invited come up with flimsy excuses for not attending what will undoubtedly be a sumptuous meal and a celebration befitting a prince and his bride. Understandably, in reading this story, typically we focus on the rude invitees who incur the king's wrath, thus leading him to tell his servants to invite to the banquet anyone they find. "So the servants went out into the streets and gathered all the people they could find, the bad as well as the good, and the wedding hall was filled with guests." (Mt. 22:10)

And so the "bad as well as the good" get to experience the undeserved grace of their king, which undoubtedly includes food prepared by what we can safely assume are the best chefs in the land. And perhaps we can indulge ourselves and further assume the meal was served buffet style. (Yes, this is a stretch, but stay with us.) Here you are, having laden your plate with the quality and quantity of food you were never expecting, heading back to your seat when an unruly nine-year-old bumps into you from behind. You stumble and drop your plate. The meal you had so looked forward to is now on the floor and you're embarrassed (you're in the presence of the king, after all) and bitterly disappointed that your carefully selected morsels now lie on the floor as the other diners carefully try to walk around them. Before you can recover, however, one of the angelic-looking servants is by your side, saying, "Not to worry, we'll take care of this; please go back and get another plate."

So it is with God's grace. There's always more at the table. And whether we dropped our plate because of our own clumsiness or

75

Gordon S. Jackson

inattentiveness to what's going on around us or the equivalent of an outside force like that unruly nine-year-old, there's always more awaiting us at the King's table.

Then, as you return with your second plate, to your even more intense embarrassment, you trip on the step and....

76

49: Hazmat Suits and Sunglasses

As [Saul] neared Damascus on his journey, suddenly a light from heaven flashed around him. He fell to the ground and heard a voice say to him, "Saul, Saul, why do you persecute me?"

— Acts 9:3-4

Firefighters and other emergency workers at times need to put on a hazmat suit, to protect them from an encounter with dangerous chemicals or gasses. The suits need to withstand a potentially overwhelming level of toxic threats.

But perhaps there's a need for an opposite concept, a suit to protect us from an overwhelming level of goodness and holiness. Think of the various references in Exodus to Moses' encounters with God. Even though God says He meets with this leader "face to face," (Ex. 32:11) we read a few verses on that mere mortals like Moses cannot see God, the pure embodiment of goodness and holiness, and live. (Ex. 33:20) When Moses asks to see God's glory the Lord offers him a compromise: "Then the Lord said, 'There is a place near me where you may stand on a rock. When my glory passes by, I will put you in a cleft in the rock and cover you with my hand until I have passed by. Then I will remove my hand and you will see my back; but my face must not be seen.'" (Ex. 33:22-23)

Might there have been special clothing that God could have given Moses for the occasion, to allow him to see even His face, a spacesuit-like garment that would have shielded him from pure goodness in the way a firefighter is shielded from toxicity? Or how about a pair of heaven-made sunglasses to cope with the brilliant light (something Paul could have used on the road to Damascus)? Apparently not; not even Moses, the godliest of men, was afforded a full view of God and no special equipment would have changed that.

Presumably conditions in heaven will be radically different. Somehow, we'll not only be able to cope with what in our earthly existence would be the overpowering presence of God and His terrifying holiness, we'll flourish in it. And protective clothing and special sunglasses to shield us from His glory won't be needed after all.

50: The Healer

He could not do any miracles there, except lay his hands on a few sick people and heal them. He was amazed at their lack of faith.

— Mark 6:5-6

Once upon a time there was prophet in a far-away land who had remarkable gifts of healing. People brought all their illnesses and infirmities before him, and out of his love for everyone he healed them all. He turned no one away. They brought him their cancers and their heart problems, their failing livers and their emphysema.

They began to bring him other problems too, like the young man who brought his low self-esteem, but could not afford counseling. So the prophet healed him right away. Then there was the young woman who came to him and said, "I want to develop a more authentic self." And her too did he heal. Once there was a man who brought his laptop computer, which was sorely troubled and could not be hooked up to his home network. The man told the prophet that he had spent many, many hours on the phone trying to get tech support, but without success. The prophet placed his hand on the laptop and said, "Go, try it now. Your faith has made it whole."

A rich man came to him one day, asking the prophet to heal his battered and bruised investment portfolio. "It took a terrible beating when the housing and financial markets collapsed," he said. "While I once had much, now I have little," he said. And the people who were in the crowd asked the prophet, "Was it this man's greed or that of his parents that caused his portfolio to suffer?"

The prophet did not answer, for his heart was heavy. He walked away, shaking the dust off his feet. As he did so, several in the crowd called after him, "And could you do something about these dirt roads?"

51: Heavenly Arrival

There are many rooms in my Father's house. If it were not so, I would have told you. I am going away to make a place for you.

— John 14:2

Every time you get back from a trip away from home there's mopping up to do: sorting the mail, unpacking one's luggage and dealing with the laundry, mowing the lawn perhaps, and putting away the suitcases. None of that will be needed on our arrival in heaven. Although it's impossible for us to imagine what that will entail, we can expect at least two things. One is a welcome of unimaginable proportions, as we're ushered into our ultimate home. The second is a sense of goodness and rightness, of belonging, that all is well.

We'll be given resurrection bodies and we'll be given resurrection minds that can cope with the new reality of eternity, a state beyond time as we now know it. Philosopher Peter Kreeft in his book *Heaven* describes how we time-bound people may quietly fear what we think will be the boredom of eternity. But that is to misunderstand the nature of time in the new dimension that will constitute heaven. Boredom will be an impossibility, he says. But however we spend our time, whatever form it takes, it's unlikely we'll need to worry about the laundry.

52: Heavy Duty Theology and the Marriage Analogy

May God himself, the God of peace, sanctify you through and through.
— 1 Thessalonians 5:23

Two important concepts that elicit much discussion among theologians are justification and sanctification. The first concerns our relationship with God and how our status is changed from sinners who, like the prodigal son, have turned our backs on our Father — only to have that relationship restored when we repent and believe in Jesus. Notice it's a change in status; we are now no longer outcasts but fully members of God's family, as Paul indicates in Romans 8. We are God's children and therefore His heirs. (Rom. 8:17)

Some of us can point to a specific moment in time when we made a commitment to Christ and changed our status to "Christian." Others of us, who have perhaps grown up in a Christian home, do not have a clear awareness of when we "became" Christians. We have known nothing else, just as we have no clear recollection of when we became our parents' child. But there's no disputing our status as God's children.

The second term, sanctification, is the process of becoming more holy and more Christ-like as we live out our faith. One writer describes it as "the process to which new life is imparted to the believer by the Holy Spirit and He is released from the compulsive power of sin and guilt and is enabled to love God and serve his neighbor."[45] In other words, we become better people, increasingly like the people God intended us to be.

So what does this have to do with marriage? Remembering yet again that no analogy is perfect, we can see justification as paralleling the day we get married. Our status has undergone a major change. However, we're not inwardly any different from what we were the day before. That is about to change. Assuming we've entered into a happy, enriching and mutually loving relationship, we expect we will grow and mature as a partner in this marriage. Slowly, over the months and years, our commitment to our partner will shape us and make us better people. As with sanctification, it's a long road. We don't become holy overnight; nor do we grow into the best possible marriage partner overnight. We need to

---

[45] Source unknown.

remember, though, that it is our status as children of God that makes possible the growth in holiness. It's not the other way around; we don't "earn" our good standing with God by working hard at being better, more holy people. Or, as Martin Luther says elsewhere, "We are not Christians because we do good works; we do good works because we are Christians."[46] We could reword that to say, "We do not become Christians by doing good works; we do good works, and become holier people, because we are Spirit-empowered Christians." Nor do we, as single people, spend years trying to be a good enough husband or wife and eventually feel we've progressed enough that we are ready to marry. What silliness! Just as our new spouse accepts us as we are, so too does God say, "Of course I know you're imperfect and need extra tutoring in Holiness 101. Ready to begin?"

---

[46] Quoted in Gordon S. Jackson: *Quotes for the Journey, Wisdom for the Way.*

53: Holy-Gifts

But such holy-gifts as you may have and the gifts you have vowed you must bring to the place which the Lord will choose.

— *Deuteronomy* 12:26, Revised English Bible

~~~~~

[But King David replied] I will not offer burnt offerings to the Lord my God which cost me nothing.

— *2 Samuel* 24:24

A creative director at a top Madison Avenue ad agency, so the story goes, suddenly got landed with a major job, which needed a fast turnaround. He turned to two of his copywriters and after briefing them on the project told them to get to work.

When they handed him their work at the end of the day, he put it in his briefcase for the long commute back home to Connecticut. The next morning, he spoke to them as soon as they arrived, asking, "Is this the best you could do?" They replied that he hadn't given them much time.

"Well, do it again, and do it right," he said. So they went back to work. Again they gave him what they'd written at the end of the day. The story was repeated: he brought back their work the next morning and said, "Look, you guys are among the highest paid copywriters in the business. Is this your best work?" Once more, they protested how little time they'd had, and got to work once more.

Finally, when he approached them on the third morning, he asked, "Have you really done your best?" Frustrated, they replied, "Yes, we have." And the creative director said, "Good; I'll take a look at it then."

~~~~~

Just as the ad man insisted on his colleagues' best work, and wouldn't bother with reading anything that wasn't, so too does God expect of us our best—whether in our faithfulness, our obedience to His will, or in our worship. Which brings us to the "holy-gifts" mentioned in the Deuteronomy reading above, according to the imaginative *Revised English Bible* translation. (Other translations use terms like "holy things," "holy offerings," or "sacred offerings.")

A true gift is something given freely, without expectation of repayment later; typically it is given out of love or respect for the recipient. But when that gift is given to God Himself, it takes on a unique status that warrants it being called a "holy-gift."

Just how significant is the nature of the gifts we bring God is underscored in the words of King David, when he says he will not offer God a sacrifice that really isn't a sacrifice at all, something that has cost him nothing.

Think of the gifts you typically give God. Are they heart-felt or tokens? Holy or routine? Genuinely sacrificial, as David insisted, or merely convenient? If God asked, "Have you given Me your best?" how would you answer?

54: Holy Hardware and the Psalms

The Lord is my rock, my fortress and my deliverer;
my God is my rock, in whom I take refuge,
my shield and the horn of my salvation, my stronghold.

— *Psalm 18:2*

Large hardware stores like Home Depot and Lowe's are fascinating places, providing solutions to countless needs and problems—many of which you've never even thought of. You can browse for hours, if you're so inclined, looking at everything from the right treatment for your lawncare needs, to the right kind of screws among dozens on offer that's perfect for your project. You can get doorknobs and power tools, toilet seats and concrete blocks for landscaping.

However, you won't find an answer to your deeper needs or problems: your chronic unhappiness or the cracks in your marriage. ("'Marital issues'? Yes, see aisle 16, next to 'Identity crises.'") Or your most fundamental need of all, a right relationship with your Maker. With that relationship secured, you know you can then bring every other issue to your heavenly Father.

Whatever your need, you can be sure the psalmist has covered it. The psalms, in effect, are God's Holy Hardware store. To take but one example, let's look at Psalm 16. We read how God provides safety and refuge, secures for the psalmist "good things," and gives him boundary lines that "have fallen for me in pleasant places." And there's more.

Keep me safe, my God,
for in you I take refuge.
I say to the Lord, "You are my Lord;
apart from you I have no good thing."
I say of the holy people who are in the land,
"They are the noble ones in whom is all my delight."
Those who run after other gods will suffer more and more.
I will not pour out libations of blood to such gods
or take up their names on my lips.
Lord, you alone are my portion and my cup;
You make my lot secure.
The boundary lines have fallen for me in pleasant places;
surely I have a delightful inheritance.
I will praise the Lord, who counsels me;

even at night my heart instructs me.
I keep my eyes always on the Lord.
With him at my right hand, I will not be shaken.
Therefore my heart is glad and my tongue rejoices;
my body also will rest secure,
because you will not abandon me to the realm of the dead,
nor will you let your faithful one see decay.
You make known to me the path of life;
You will fill me with joy in your presence,
with eternal pleasures at your right hand.

Or how about where the psalmist lists a string of solutions to his need for safety and security:
The Lord is my rock, my fortress and my deliverer;
my God is my rock, in whom I take refuge,
my shield and the horn of my salvation, my stronghold. (Ps. 18:2)

Either re-read Psalm 16 or one of your favorite psalms. Read it afresh, looking for assurance in facing any problems and needs today.

55: The Holy Spirit and the Rheostat

In the same way, the Spirit helps us in our weakness. We do not know what we ought to pray for, but the Spirit himself intercedes for us through wordless groans.

— Romans 8:26

Think of that light in your living room with the variable switch. You can raise or lower the switch, brightening or darkening the room to suit your mood. What makes that possible is a rheostat. Time to get a bit technical, sorry. The *Chambers Dictionary* describes a rheostat as "a variable resistor that enables the resistance to a current in an electric circuit to be increased or decreased, thereby varying the current without interrupting the current flow, eg. as when dimming a light bulb."

Let's unpack these elements one by one. Instead of talking about a "resistor," however, we'll flip this over and use the term "facilitator," as in the Holy Spirit. And the current is the power of the Spirit working within us. We, of course, are the light bulb.

What then is this "variable" bit all about? Well, there's reason to believe that the power of the Spirit within us is not only an "uninterrupted" presence but that His role in our lives also varies according to our needs. For example, as J. B. Phillips translates it, Jesus tells His disciples what to expect in a time of persecution: "But when they are taking you off to trial, do not worry beforehand about what you are going to say—simply say the words you are given when the time comes. For it is not really you who will speak, but the Holy Spirit." (Mk. 13:11, *Phillips*)

Then, in Paul's letter to the Romans we read: "In the same way, the Spirit helps us in our weakness. We do not know what we ought to pray for, but the Spirit himself intercedes for us through wordless groans." (Rom. 8:26) Clearly, as our needs vary, so the Spirit's support varies to meet the occasion. But regardless of our theology of the Holy Spirit we can be sure of two things. One is that the Spirit is intimately involved in our lives. The other is that even when our light shines most dimly, when life is the pits and everything seems to have fallen apart, there is still that faint glow, as we are sustained by the Spirit's energy coursing through us.

56: Hounded

For this is what the Sovereign LORD says: I myself will search for my sheep and look after them.

— Ezekiel 34:11

You may not have been aware of it, but you have your very own spiritual sheep dog, says Gerard Hughes. He says it keeps scurrying around you, trying to drive you toward God. "When we try to satisfy ourselves with something that is not leading us to God, then we feel dissatisfied, bored, empty and frustrated, which is the harrying of the sheep dog."[47] He adds, "That is why our negative feelings of sadness, anxiety, agitation, etc. can be so important: they can be telling us that our direction is wrong."

Call it your conscience, or that natural void in your life where you still haven't let God take full possession. Francis Thompson's famous poem, "The Hound of Heaven," describes his experience of God harrying him relentlessly, sheep-dog style, until he finally found himself in God's presence and committed his life to Him. The poem begins, "I fled Him down the nights and down the days. I fled Him down the arches of the years...." As he discovered, God's sheep dog neither tires nor quits.

Same with each of us. Perhaps you don't believe that we each have a guardian angel, but it could be we have a guardian sheep dog, which also never tires nor quits.

---

[47] Gerard Hughes: *God of Surprises*.

87

57: Hubert Humphrey and the High-Schooler

You have searched me, Lord, and you know me. You know when I sit and when I rise; you perceive my thoughts from afar. You discern my going out and my lying down; you are familiar with all my ways.

— Psalm 139:1-3

Hubert Horatio Humphrey was a gregarious Minnesota politician, who served his state for five terms as a US Senator. But he is best known for serving as Lyndon Johnson's vice president, from 1965 to 1969, and his narrow loss to Richard Nixon in the 1968 presidential election.

His reputation as a strongly people-oriented politician continued up to his premature death at age sixty-six, of bladder cancer. While still receiving treatment in the hospital before returning home to die, he walked around the wards telling jokes to other patients and listening to their concerns.

One episode perfectly captures his outgoing spirit. During his presidential campaign, he briefly visited a Minnesota high school. A student approached him and asked if he'd do a taped interview for the school's radio station. Humphrey agreed, to the irritation of his campaign staffers. There was no political advantage to be gained from a high school radio interview, all the more so because this was in his home state, one he was certain to win.

The student, thrilled to have this journalistic coup, then recorded Humphrey for about thirty to forty minutes, to the growing impatience of his aides. The interview concluded, and on checking her recorder she realized, to her horror, something had gone wrong and she had nothing. So Humphrey did the entire interview again.

~~~~~

The story reflects the character of a politician who, while running for the highest office in the land, was willing to commit a chunk of time, and then double that commitment, to a "nobody," a high-schooler who was too young to vote. (Eighteen-year-olds got that right only in 1971.)

We read repeatedly in the Old Testament how God called Abraham and his offspring to form a nation, the children of Israel. In the New Testament, we hear again and again Jesus speaking of the Kingdom of God. Paul writes about the church as the Body of Christ, another collection of people. Yet we must never forget that nations, kingdoms, and churches are made up of individuals, each invaluable to God, each made in His image. Each of us, Jesus assures us, is known to God individually: "Indeed, the very hairs of your head are all numbered. Don't be afraid; you are worth more than many sparrows." (Lk. 12:7)

Then there's the psalmist, who says, "You have searched me, Lord, and You know me. You know when I sit and when I rise; You perceive my thoughts from afar. You discern my going out and my lying down; You are familiar with all my ways." (Ps. 139:1-3)

Or how about Moses, whom God called as an individual to lead His people out of Egypt, and of whom He says, "I know you by name." (Ex. 33:17)

None of us is a Moses. One thing we have in common with him, however, is that God knows us too by name. And like that Minnesota high-schooler decades ago, we too receive individual, undivided attention, giving us all the time we want.

58: An Infectious Laugh

He will yet fill your mouth with laughter and your lips with shouts of joy.
— Job 8:21

In the wake of COVID 19, we may be hesitant to use the phrase, "an infectious laugh." That would be a pity, because those words describe someone with a joyous, inviting laugh that draws us into the merriment of the moment. You find that you can't help yourself laughing along with the person, all the more so because the source of an infectious laugh is invariably someone with an irresistible, magnetic joy that draws you in — not against your will, but with an eagerness to be within this person's orbit.

And that, when you think about it, is what Christians should be like, if we take seriously what Jesus said: "I have told you this so that my joy may be in you and that your joy may be complete." (Jn. 15:11) We have on offer the joy of Christ Himself, the sinless One, who personifies all that is good. We're talking here about a man whose charisma drew even the little children to him.

But what of Christians who seem devoid of the joy that Jesus promised? George Gurdjieff (1886-1949) was a charismatic spiritual teacher, mystic and philosopher, who was active mostly in Europe and the United States. At one point he ran a commune in France, whose participants paid to join. One of these was a notoriously difficult old man, "irritable, messy, fighting with everyone, and unwilling to clean up or help in any manner. No one was able to get along with him."[48]

Eventually, the man decided to leave the group, but Gurdjieff went after him to persuade him to return. No, said the man. It had been too difficult for him. Then Gurdjieff made him an offer he couldn't refuse: he'd pay him a generous salary to rejoin the group. When the man came back, the others were appalled, especially because he was now being paid while they were charged to be there. When they complained to Gurdjieff, he gathered them together and explained his thinking: "This old man is like yeast for bread. Without him here you would never really learn about anger, irritability, patience and compassion. That is why you pay me and I hire him."

This person is like the surly woman who ran a Christian bookstore,

---

[48] This story is told in John Marks Templeton, *Worldwide Laws of Life*.

of whom a customer said, "It's a good thing she sells Bibles; she couldn't sell anything else." Even those customers who'd stopped off to buy a Bible or other Christian literature went there reluctantly.

What, you are entitled to ask, accounts for the joylessness in this woman and the man in the commune? It could be any of a dozen reasons. Bearing in mind the bumper sticker that says, "Be patient—God isn't finished with me yet," one hopes for growth and improvement in folks like these. Meanwhile, one might wonder what it is about their faith that leaves them so joyless. Perhaps they haven't taken to heart the words of Pierre Teilhard de Chardin, who said: "Joy is the surest sign of the presence of God."[49] And in case you hadn't noticed, joyful people laugh a lot, in a way that is wonderfully contagious.

[49] https://quotepark.com/quotes/921731-pierre-teilhard-de-chardin-joy-is-the-infallible-sign-of-the-presence-of-god/. Accessed Sept. 4, 2023.

59: Install and Reboot

Show me your faith without deeds, and I will show you my faith by my deeds. You believe that there is one God. Good! Even the demons believe that — and shudder. You foolish person, do you want evidence that faith without deeds is useless?

— James 2:18-20

You've installed a new piece of software and it's ready to roll. Well, almost. You get the instruction to reboot your computer for it to take effect.

The apostle James would understand this two-step process. He wrote, "Show me your faith without deeds, and I will show you my faith by my deeds. You believe that there is one God. Good! Even the demons believe that — and shudder. You foolish person, do you want evidence that faith without deeds is useless?" (Jms. 2:18-20) Install without rebooting? It's useless.

It's all good and well to make a Christian commitment; that's an indispensable first step. Yet by itself it isn't enough until we've begun living out this new "program" that we've loaded. Or to extend the analogy, it's more like an entirely new operating system that we've installed, rather than only a program. For the operating system governs everything else that happens on the computer, just like the fundamental reorientation of our lives once we commit ourselves to Christ. We now think differently and should live differently.

As with our computer, we're still going to encounter glitches along the way. That's the time to reboot yet again, setting everything back to where it should be. The spiritual equivalent is repentance.

Before this analogy gets out of control, however, let's return to James' warning. His caution is plain: Without deeds flowing out of our faith, a spiritual reboot is clearly in order.

60: Job Shadowing God for a Day

Great is our Lord and mighty in power; his understanding has no limit.
— Psalm 147:5

In your teens or twenties, you may have spent a day following someone to get a sense of what his or her job entailed. Perhaps an actuary, advertising executive, or architect. Or a banker, biologist, or bookkeeper. Your goal was to explore what this person actually did on a day-to-day basis and learn whether those activities appealed to you as a possible career. Having accepted you as a shadow for the day, that person would presumably also be generous enough with his or her time to squeeze in conversations about the rewards and downsides of the job.

But let's engage in the thought experiment of imagining that God has invited you to shadow Him for a day, to learn what a typical "work day" (if there is such a thing) looks like for Him. No, you're not deluded enough to think you could aspire to becoming God, as you could an actuary, advertising executive, or architect. But what insights might you glean by imagining you are in God's presence from 9 to 5 next Monday? (And this includes an hour's break where He takes you to lunch to discuss what you've been observing.)

~~~~~

Get a sheet of paper and list five or more things you can imagine that bring God joy, in His role as Lord God, the Holy One who is creator and sustainer of all things. Next, list five things that grieve Him. Then, push this further, as you imagine that you've taken notes during your one-on-one lunchtime conversation with Him. What did He tell you about being God?

93

61: Keyboarding Gone Etpmh

The one who is victorious will, like them, be dressed in white. I will never blot out the name of that person from the book of life, but will acknowledge that name before my Father and his angels.

— Revelation 3:5

Oops, that should be "Keyboarding Gone *Wrong*." Sorry. I was only one letter off; inadvertently, I let my hands shift one letter to the right. Only a small mistake, really—only one letter, as I said. I was close, wasn't I?

When I was learning to type, in a six-week course I took before college, our instructor kept talking about the need to anchor our fingers over the right keys. Let your fingers drift, even one key, you'd be in trouble.

~~~~~

"It was just one little sin, Lord—merely a white lie."

"So how could cheating on my MCATs to get into med school really be a bad thing? You know my heart, Lord, and that I'm committed to serve You on the mission field."

"Okay, maybe strictly speaking I shouldn't have over-valued those charitable donations on my tax forms. But I pay enough in taxes as it is and everyone else gets creative as well—and from the water cooler chatter at work it's obvious they fiddle the government out of a lot more."

~~~~~

"Okay, so I was only a little off on what You expected of me, Lord. Is that really a problem? What's that You say, Lord? You've noticed that my name in Your Book of Life is a little off? Yes, it should be Anders, Dave Anders. And all You can find is 'Fsbr Smfrtd'? Just one key off. But You say there's a way to fix that, Lord....?"

62: King Clovis' Troops

No one can serve two masters.

– Matthew 6:24

It was the year 496 and King Clovis of the Franks, a pagan, was in deep trouble on his home turf in Gaul. He was under attack by German troops and was losing ground. Desperate, he thought of his wife's Christian faith and prayed, "Jesus, if you really are the Son of God as my wife tells me, grant me victory and I will believe in you."[50]

Miraculously, the tide turned and the German troops fled. True to his word, Clovis converted and was baptized. Moreover, he required his 3,000 soldiers to convert as well. At their mass baptism, however, the troops weren't entirely sure about what they were committing too. The story is that many of them, when they went under the water, held their weapons above the surface, indicating their unwillingness to subject their soldiering role to God's authority. Their partial immersion reflected either an equally incomplete theology, or the conscripted character of their supposed conversion, or both.

~~~~~

Almost all the readers of this book will have been baptized, in one way or another, perhaps as infants or perhaps as an older person who was presumably aware of the symbolism of baptism. Either way, the unhappy example of Clovis' army and their "holding-back-baptism" holds a lesson for us more than 1,500 years later. God wants an authentic relationship with His people. He doesn't like half-hearted commitments or any attempts at playing games.

As we've noted elsewhere, in James' epistle he warns against believers who are "double minded." He uses an interesting Greek word, δίψυχος, which literally means "two souled." James describes such a person as "unstable in all they do." (Jms. 1:8) Sounds like the divided loyalties of Clovis' army. They may have been loyal to King Clovis but how much God could count on them was another matter. Jesus had it right when He said, "No one can serve two masters." (Mt. 6:24)

---

[50] https://www.christianity.com/church/church-history/timeline/301-600/king-clovis-took-to-the-water-11629704.html#:~:text=A%20contingent%20of%20Germans%20was,victory%20to%20the%20Christian%20God. Accessed Sept. 4, 2023.

63:The Kitka Loaf

But whoever is united with the Lord is one with him in spirit.
—1 Corinthians 6:17

A kitka is a braided loaf, also known as challah bread, traditionally part of the Jewish sabbath. Describing her memories of growing up observing the sabbath, one Jewish writer recalled how following an opening prayer, the loaf was passed around. Everyone would break off a piece of the bread and perhaps add a dash of salt before eating it.

Besides the sheer pleasure of the bread's freshness, a kitka offers something else: a reminder during this sabbath meal that the braids signify our intertwined oneness with God. By definition, a kitka is made up of two strands of dough (occasionally more, if the baker is ambitious). They are baked together, becoming one unit, just as we become united with Christ, as Paul indicates in several places[51]

Similarly, it is impossible to separate out one strand and still have a kitka. God has chosen to entwine Himself with us, choosing to use us so that together we may feed those who hunger for sabbath bread.

---

[51] See for example 1 Corinthians 6:17 and Philippians 2:1.

64: Know Who You're Dealing With

For the LORD your God is God of gods and Lord of lords, the great God, mighty and awesome....

– Deuteronomy 10:17

Harrods department store in England wanted to expand its footprint on a city block but faced a problem: a small chapel stood in their way. So, as J. Clif Christopher tells the story in his book *Rich Church, Poor Church*, the directors wrote to the chapel's leadership. Their letter stated, "The Board of Directors at Harrods has determined that it is in our best interest to expand next year. We are prepared to offer you a fair market price for your little chapel and even include additional capital to assist you in relocation." The letter asked for a reply within two weeks.

They heard back from the chapel's board of directors within a week. The reply noted that the chapel had occupied the site for more than a hundred years, adding: "We have recently determined that it is in our best interest to expand next year. Your department store occupies the site we want to use for our expansion. We are prepared to offer you a fair market price for your store and even throw in additional capital to assist you in relocation."

The Harrods directors initially thought the letter was a spoof of what they had sent—until they saw who had signed the letter: John Cadbury, founder of the Cadbury company, which initially sold tea, coffee and hot chocolate before becoming one of the world's best-known manufacturers of chocolate and other candy. Cadbury, a devout Quaker, was a member of the chapel and one of England's richest men, well able to back the chapel's offer to buy out the department store.

It would have helped Harrods' directors if they had known in advance who they were dealing with. Likewise with anyone who is up against God's people. Let's visit for a moment the story of Elisha and his bewildered servant:

> *When the servant of the man of God got up and went out early the next morning, an army with horses and chariots had surrounded the city. "Oh no, my lord! What shall we do?" the servant asked. "Don't be afraid," the prophet answered. "Those who are with us are more than those who are with them." And Elisha prayed, "Open his eyes, Lord, so that he may see." Then the Lord opened the servant's eyes, and he looked and saw the hills full of horses and*

chariots of fire all around Elisha. (2 Kng 6:15-17)

What is going on with Elisha? His capacity for seeing a more complete reality far outstripped that of his servant. We can only marvel at the depth of faith and spirituality that enabled him to see things that almost all believers cannot. Even those of us who speak most fervently of our "Christian worldview" must concede that we do not see with Elisha's supra-human spiritual clarity. To be honest, we would seek psychiatric help for a loved one facing a life crisis, as Elisha did, who spoke of seeing invisible forces of help, whether these were the police, the military, or a high-powered legal team.

The king of Aram, who was at war with Israel and at this moment had Elisha in his sights, had completely disregarded the possibility that his opponent might have had invisible, divine resources, against which the king's impressive army didn't have a hope.

Or take Jesus' comment in the Garden of Gethsemane, when He admonishes the disciple who drew a sword to attack the arresting party: "Do you think I cannot call on my Father, and he will at once put at my disposal more than twelve legions of angels?" (Mt. 26:53)

Who knows what resources, invisible to the naked eye of Elisha's servant, or in reserve, should God's will call for their use, are available to us too? Few of us have the wealth of a John Cadbury. But each of us can address the challenges or even outright opposition we face in our response. And if we were writing a letter, as John Cadbury did, we could conclude with our signature, representing the One who has our back.

65: Learned Helplessness

[E]ven the darkness will not be dark to you; the night will shine like the day, for darkness is as light to you.

— Psalm 139:12

The concept of learned helplessness came into psychology in the middle of last century. At the risk of oversimplifying it, the idea is that if people repeatedly experience a negative and stressful situation that is beyond their control, they may reach the point where they give up trying to deal with it.

The Medical News Today website says, "Once a person having this experience discovers that they cannot control events around them, they lose motivation. Even if an opportunity arises that allows the person to alter their circumstances, they do not take action."[52] The site gives as an example someone who has tried repeatedly to stop smoking but failed; he or she eventually concludes that it will never happen and is resigned to accepting it will never happen. Or think of a schoolchild volunteering the answer to a question and told by the teacher that her answer is wrong. Same with the child's next answer. And the third. Soon enough, the child is going to stop volunteering, convinced that she is a poor student. If this occurred over an extended period, the child may well withdraw into herself and define herself as a failure—and not offer any answers at all.

The experience of repeated inability to deal with a stressful situation, like child or spouse abuse, therefore leads to an assumption of futility that may be associated with depression. An abused child, for example, whose self-esteem has been shattered may struggle to respond well to a loving situation if he is removed from his traumatic environment. Both children and adults may need extended counseling to help them overcome their learned helplessness.

We can at times find a parallel in our spiritual lives; it's termed "the dark night of the soul." [53] The term was originated by St. John of the Cross, a sixteenth-century Spanish mystic. It refers to a bleak, desolate stretch in

---

[52]https://www.medicalnewstoday.com/articles/325355#:~:text=In%20psycholo gy%2C%20learned%20helplessness%20is,opportunities%20for%20change%20bec ome%20available. Accessed Sept. 4, 2023.

[53] https://en.wikipedia.org/wiki/Dark_Night_of_the_Soul. Accessed Sept. 4, 2023.

one's spiritual life when God seems remote or even totally absent. Many prominent Christians have suffered from this ordeal, sometimes for long periods. For instance, a 2007 *Time* magazine article on Mother Teresa noted that she experienced grave doubts and spiritual darkness from 1948 more or less continuously until shortly before her death in 1997. So did Martin Luther and countless other Christians through the ages.

Their experience may not have been a *learned* helplessness, but they led to a sense of helplessness nonetheless. For by its very nature nothing seems to "work" as one tries to extricate oneself from this grim condition, something like the equivalent of depression in the spiritual realm. Prayer doesn't accomplish anything. Nor does Bible study or counseling. Nor can one "just snap out of it," as Mother Teresa and Martin Luther would tell us if they were still with us.

We may pray as earnestly as ever, yet it seems that God neither hears nor responds. As E. M. Blaiklock says, "It is one of the sternest tests of faith when God appears not to care, to be inactive, dead."[54] During these dark days it may be tempting to give up on one's faith. No doubt many have. But just as victims of learned helplessness can surmount the experiences that have dragged them down, there is hope for Christians struggling with the dark night of the soul. As Edmond Rostand said, "It is at night that faith in light is admirable."[55] A difference though is that our "daybreak" lies in God's hands, not those of therapists. Until then, we can only cling to a God Whom we assert by blind faith is good, loving, and despite the surrounding darkness, has neither forgotten nor abandoned us. Mystified though we may be at this moment at God's seeming absence, we need to reflect on what we knew before the darkness fell and heed the words of V. Raymond Edman: "Never doubt in the dark what God told you in the light."[56]

Meanwhile, if you are grappling with this kind of spiritual darkness, be alert for those glimmers of light that God may send your way. Beware of becoming so resigned to your darkness that you no longer expect God's light again, like someone with learned helplessness, and refuse to recognize "a way out" when it appears. Recall that no matter how despondent you may feel, you serve a God Who scoffs at the word "helpless."

---

[54] E. M. Blaiklock: *Handbook of Bible People.*
[55] Quoted in Gordon S. Jackson: *Quotes for the Journey, Wisdom for the Way.*
[56] Quoted in Gordon S. Jackson: *Quotes for the Journey, Wisdom for the Way.*

66: A Lesson from Leon Uris

"Why do you call me, 'Lord, Lord,' and do not do what I say?"
— *Luke 6:46*

Leon Uris (1923-2004) was an American writer best known for his novels. In one of them, *Armageddon: A Novel of Berlin* (1963), he describes one aspect of how Nazi SS officers were trained. They were each given a puppy to raise, supposedly to help the recruits learn discipline. Then, after several months, each recruit was abruptly ordered to kill the puppy. If they showed any hesitation, they were ousted from the program.

~~~~~

Whether this story has any basis in fact is disputed. Some versions say this occurred in the Hitler Youth program, which critics have said wasn't true.

But regardless of how much Uris' description is based in fact (and apparently his historical novels were well researched), this tale holds an important lesson for Christians: How ready are we to obey God's unwelcome commands? Especially the really, really unwelcome ones? (Like "I want you to go to Somalia as a missionary"?)

No, hesitation on our part won't get us kicked out of "God's program." And you may never face this kind of test. However, think of Peter and God's command to take the gospel message to Cornelius, a Gentile. It is preceded by a vision in which he's told to eat unclean food, an unwelcome command to a Jew if ever there was one. Not only does Peter hesitate, he has the audacity to tell God "no."

As we know, Peter doesn't get kicked out of the program. But at the very least God must have found his hesitation and then refusal to be tiresome.

67: Lessons from the Frogs

Do not conform to the pattern of this world, but be transformed by the renewing of your mind.

— Romans 12:2

Frogs are amphibians, living on both land and in water. They come in all kinds, about 4,800 species recorded to date — sort of like the people whom you'll see at churches across the world, as we too come in all types. Not only in size, shape, color, height and width, but in personality and politics and, to some degree, in our Christian beliefs as well. You'd probably be surprised by two things: One is how different we are; the other is how similar we are, despite those differences, in holding to a few core beliefs about God's love and the gospel message.

Secondly, like these amphibians, Christians also see ourselves as being able to live in two settings. We're focused both on God's heavenly Kingdom while living our lives in an earthly setting — of dentist appointments, soccer games, snow tires, and work. Living in both realms at the same time, we believe, makes us fully human. And while we can ask if frogs are creatures of the pond first and the land second, or the other way around, we have no doubt about our situation. Despite our ability to be both earthly and heavenly minded at the same time, we are ultimately spiritual beings. As Pierre Teilhard de Chardin says, "We are not human beings having a spiritual experience. We are spiritual beings having a human experience."[57] Not like frogs.

Finally, there's the parallel between how frogs start out as tadpoles and how Christians likewise don't start out fully formed. Some of us are new in our faith, like a tadpole. But also like a tadpole, we have the astonishing potential to grow into what we were made to be: children of God, walking in a close, day-by-day relationship with our Lord. Like the marvel of tadpoles becoming frogs, each of us is a "work in progress," as we are transformed into the "God-created someone" we've been destined to be all along.

---

[57] https://www.brainyquote.com/quotes/pierre_teilhard_de_chardi_160888. Accessed Sept. 4, 2023.

68: Like a Mighty Tortoise

I know your deeds; you have a reputation of being alive, but you are dead. Wake up! Strengthen what remains and is about to die, for I have found your deeds unfinished in the sight of my God. Remember, therefore, what you have received and heard; hold it fast, and repent.

— Revelation 3:1-3

~~~~~

Like a mighty tortoise moves the Church of God;
Brothers we are treading, where we've always trod;
We are all divided, many bodies we,
Very strong on doctrine, weak on charity.

—Source unknown

This is a parody of a verse in the hymn "Onward Christian Soldiers," by Sabine Baring-Gould, the original being:

Like a mighty army moves the church of God;
brothers, we are treading where the saints have trod.
We are not divided, all one body we,
one in hope and doctrine, one in charity.

Now, three recommended responses... First, some admiration for the unidentified writer who wittily played with the original. (Brief applause; thank you.) Second, a look at the original version and the important truths it notes about God's church and how its activities today are built on the work of the countless saints who have gone before us.

And finally, the awkward part: Ask yourself, how close is the parody to reality? What about *your* church? Are you treading where you've always trod? Are you all divided and weak on charity? How would your pastor or priest respond if you sent this to him or her? With a chuckle, indignation, or sadness?

Maybe the mighty tortoise isn't the right analogy to describe your church in action. Can you think of a creature that would more accurately describe it? Is it more like a sloth or an eagle? Is your church regarded in the community more like a powerful lion or a timid lamb? Why?

69: Look!

There once was a man, his name John, sent by God.... He came to show everyone where to look, who to believe in.

— *John 1:6-7*, The Message

~~~~~

[L]ooking is necessary for seeing — if you don't look, you can't possibly see it. But looking is not sufficient for seeing — looking at something doesn't guarantee that you will notice it.

— *Christopher Chabris & Daniel Simons*[58]

During the early morning rush hour, on a Friday in January 2007, a man with a violin took up his position as a busker among the commuters in Washington DC's L'Enfant Plaza Station. For the next forty-three minutes he played half a dozen classical pieces, for the edification of the passersby.

Virtually nobody paid any attention; he was, after all, presumably just another street musician (or "subway musician," to be precise) trying to make a few bucks. In fact, he made $32.17, according to *The Washington Post*, which reported the story.[59] Not bad, for an amateur, even a gifted one. But it was a fraction of what the violinist earned in his regular setting. For the artist was Joshua Bell, one of the world's greatest violinists, playing on his Stradivarius estimated to be worth some $3.5 million.

The exercise was part of an experiment arranged by the newspaper, with Bell's cooperation, to see how people would respond to world class artistry when yanked out of its usual context. Nobody expects to find a concert violinist busking for money in a subway station. Virtually no one did. Most rushed by en route to work.

"As it happens," though, the *Post* reported, "exactly one person recognized Bell, and she didn't arrive until near the very end. For Stacy Furukawa, a demographer at the Commerce Department, there was no doubt. She does not know much about classical music but she had been in the audience three weeks earlier, at Bell's free concert at the Library of Congress. And here he was, the international virtuoso, sawing away, begging for money. She had no idea what the heck was going on, but whatever it was, she wasn't about to miss it."[60]

---

58 Chabris and Simons, *The Invisible Gorilla*.
59 Cited in Chabris and Simons, *The Invisible Gorilla*.
60 Ibid.

Furukawa alone took the time to look and listen, and soak in the beauty, oblivious that she was part of the *Post's* experiment. The story, which won the paper a Pulitzer Prize, was titled "Pearls Before Breakfast." The story embodied Alan Watts' observation that, "Normally, we do not so much look at things as overlook them."[61] It also speaks to our perfectly human predisposition to get on with life on a busy morning's commute to work. Or getting the kids to soccer, picking up something from the supermarket, or dropping off the dry cleaning—all routine tasks, each important in its own way.

But every now and again, for the Christian, God breaks into the routine and says, "Look! Stop what you are doing. Something special is happening here; you need to pay attention." God's telling us to "Look!" is the visual equivalent of "listen up." We are given a command, perhaps quite unexpectedly. Grammatically, God speaks in the imperative. There is an urgency here. Any one of us could be told to "Look!"—and at any time. We never know when God might interrupt, tap us on the shoulder and point somewhere, and say: "Look, see what I'm doing; see what's happening in front of you!"

"Looking" is integral to our Christian walk. How we do so is of vital importance. Whoever is looking, or has looked, or is commanded to look, is doing so with a clarity of purpose; the act deserves full attention and a readiness by the "looker" to give his or her full attention. No multi-tasking permitted here.

At any moment God can break into our lives with His word to us: "Look, over here; I've got something to show you." Those moments, however, are unpredictable and for most of us, pretty rare. Nor are they under our control. What we *do* control daily is what we choose to attend to, and what we make our priorities. The "Look!" moments by definition are unexpected. When they come, we need to be ready to look as we participate in God's unexpectedly wondrous plans for our lives. As John B. Taylor asked, "How much adventure is there in my faith? Or am I sitting at home eating pomegranates?"[62]

---

[61] Quoted in John Lloyd and John Mitchinson, *If Ignorance is Bliss.*
[62] Scripture Union Bible reading notes, *Encounter with God.* Date unknown.

70: Marathon Man

... let us run with perseverance the race marked out for us.
— Hebrews 12:1

Legendary Kenyan long-distance runner Eliud Kipchoge, the marathon gold medal winner at the 2016 and 2020 Olympics, also holds the world record, set in 2018. But it's his run the following year that interests us.

In October 2019, he became the first person to run a marathon in less than two hours. But the astonishing feat wasn't eligible to merit world record status for a simple reason: it wasn't a real race, the event having been arranged specifically to see if he could break the iconic two-hour mark. A team of thirty-six runners pushed him to run an average of 4:33:5 minutes per mile — leaving him to cover the last 500 meters on his own. He finished twenty seconds under the two-hour mark. Two other factors helping him were a new type of Nike shoe that gave him an extra edge, and the carefully chosen flat course: the Prater Park, in Vienna, where the trees protected him from the wind.

The event was set up, in other words, not so much as a race but as a test: to see if he could break the two-hour barrier on a special course with every possible advantage. And therein lies a lesson for us. The writer of Hebrews tells us, "let us run with perseverance the race marked out for us." (Heb. 12:1) Like Kipchoge, we have a course marked out for us, set up by a God Who seeks to give us every possible advantage and resource. But so often we don't take advantage of what God seeks to make available to us. As God says through the prophet Malachi, "Test me ... and see if I don't open up heaven itself to you and pour out blessings beyond your wildest dreams." (Mal. 3:10, *The Message*)

God knows our circumstances, strengths, weaknesses, and readiness to serve. In response, He tailors the course we are to run according to our individual needs. Your course may be similar to mine, but not identical. Or, because of who you are, it may differ in significant ways. Regardless, God assures us of every advantage, beginning with the psalmist's assurance that those of us who seek to walk godly lives are "like a tree planted by streams of water." (Ps. 1:3)

Having begun to mix our metaphors, with trees running the race God has set before us, let's add one more. Matthew Henry says, "God knows what He designs for us, that we be furnished with grace sufficient.

He that appoints what the voyage shall be will victual [supply] the ship accordingly."[63] However we see our journey, then, by land or sea, we can be assured that we have a God Who is passionately seeking our success in the race marked out for us.

Equipping us for the journey and clearing the pathway does not mean an obstacle-free life, however. God is not a "curlingfiorde parent," a wonderful Danish term relying on the image, from the sport of curling, of a parent who scurries ahead of a child to smooth away every possible obstacle. The New Testament is rife with references to the difficulties we must expect in life, including at times even suffering for our faith. But we can be assured that our equivalent of Eliud Kipchoge's carefully chosen course in Vienna is optimally designed for us. Nobody said running that course would be easy. Like running a regular marathon, for that matter...

---

[63] Matthew Henry: *One Volume Commentary on the Bible.*

71: Mayor La Guardia Remembers

For we do not have a high priest who is unable to empathize with our
weaknesses, but we have one who has been tempted in every way, just as we are....
— *Hebrews 4:15*

When he was mayor of New York, Fiorella La Guardia at one point thought the city's police were being too harsh in dealing with young offenders.[64] He "tried to point out to them the difference between a mischievous prank and true juvenile delinquency." To make his point, he told the officers, "When I was a boy I used to wander around the streets with my friends until we found a horse tied up to a post. We'd unhitch him, ride him around town, then tie him up again."

One of the officers asked, "Are you trying to tell us that the mayor of New York was once a horse thief?"

"No," the mayor replied. "I'm telling you that he was once a boy."

~~~~~

And Jesus tells us that He remembers what it was like to live out an earthly existence, experiencing all the things we do: from hunger and hurt, to knowing human love and that of His heavenly Father; from friendship to betrayal. Jesus tells us that He too was once a boy, and one of us.

At times of crisis, we may have some well-intentioned friend come beside us and say, "I know how you feel." Yet you know they don't have a clue what you're going through. But if it's someone who has shared an experience with you — the loss of a spouse or a child, drug addiction or alcoholism, the loss of a job — ah, now we know that they can relate to us and our plight. And Jesus' incarnation qualifies Him to relate to our human nature because He is no distant, impersonal God. Zeus or Baal could never identify with or empathize with you and me; it took the miracle of God incarnate to do that. For Jesus was once a babe, then a boy, then a man — one of us.

---

[64] This story is recounted in *The Little Brown Book of Anecdotes*, ed. Clifton Fadiman.

72: Only a Limited Time

My times are in your hands....

— Psalm 31:15

In one key respect, Pat Borgens personified one aspect of the Christian life: its transitoriness. She served the Billy Graham organization for twelve years as a member of the advance team that would go from one city to another to prepare for the evangelist's crusades. Typically, she said, the team would spend a year in a city, nine months training volunteers and making other arrangements, and three months afterwards ensuring appropriate follow-up for anyone who needed it.

Moving to the next venue meant finding a place to stay for all the advance team members, which included finding suitable rental properties. When spelling out their needs, they'd make clear they were going to be in town for only a limited time. They weren't interested in buying, thank you.

~~~~~

Christians generally need to see themselves as being "in town" for only a limited time. In the words of the song by Jim Reeves, "This world is not my home, I'm just a passing through...." To be sure, just as with the Billy Graham advance teams, there's work to be done while we're here. But this is not our primary home and not the place to commit ourselves to buying a house. Like Pat Borgens, we may find ourselves needing to move on from this city to the next, where new work awaits us. But always we're to see ourselves as being in town for only a limited time, ready to move on to our next assignment. Spiritually speaking, we are only renters.

One biblical example of such flexibility is found in Philip and his encounter with the Ethiopian eunuch, recorded in Acts chapter 8. After encountering this high-ranking official, Philip is invited into the man's chariot to help him understand what he is reading in the book of Isaiah. But then, after baptizing the man, we read one of the strangest passages in the New Testament: "When they came up out of the water, the Spirit of the Lord suddenly took Philip away, and the eunuch did not see him again, but went on his way rejoicing. Philip, however, appeared at Azotus and traveled about, preaching the gospel in all the towns until he reached Caesarea." (Acts 8:39-40) His particular missionary assignment with the official now completed, God mysteriously whisks him away for other assignments.

Few of us, if any, will experience such a dramatic move, and almost certainly not to Azotus. Some of us are going to be placed in one setting for the rest of our lives. Benedictine monks, for example, include in their vows a commitment to "stability," the idea that they will stay with this group of monks, in this place, for the rest of their days.

For some of us, our earthly stay is like that of Pat Borgens, moving from one city to the next to do God's work. For others, either by choice or by default, we will stay in one place, like the Benedictines. For all of us, though, we need to have the mindset that we are just passing through. Or, as British writer Malcolm Muggeridge put it, "The only ultimate disaster than can befall us is to feel ourselves at home on this earth."[65]

---

[65] Quoted in Gordon S. Jackson: *Quotes for the Journey, Wisdom for the Way*.

73: The Painter

The servant came back and reported this to his master. Then the owner of the house became angry and ordered his servant, "Go out quickly into the streets and alleys of the town and bring in the poor, the crippled, the blind and the lame."
— Luke 14:21

The story is told of one of those genius painters during the Italian renaissance who was working on his next masterpiece. He needed a model, ideally a young boy of nine or ten, with a waif-like look. He spent hours scouring the marketplace where people gathered until he finally identified a child who would be perfect for the painting he envisaged: The child was grubby, with tousled blond hair, poorly clothed, and with a naïvely innocent expression.

The painter told the boy's mother that he wanted the boy to pose for him over a number of weeks, and that he'd pay so much up front and the rest upon completion of the sittings. The mother agreed, took the initial payment, and agreed to bring her ten-year-old son to the painter's studio on Monday at 9 a.m.

Monday came, and so did the mother and child. However, she had taken the initial payment to buy the boy new clothing, scrubbed his face till it was spotless, and perfectly groomed his hair. She wanted her son to look his best. Gone was the appearance of the waif the painter had seen, and so was the boy's earlier expression. Dressed up as he was, his face now exuded a look of pride and self-confidence that was of no use to the painter.

Disappointed, the painter explained to the woman why he could no longer use her son as a model. Her best intentions had ruined the painter's plan. He paid her a few more coins and sent her on her way.

~~~~~

As you look to the next steps on your journey, you wonder in your more earnest moments how God could use someone like you. Despite your best intentions, you stumble into sin. You struggle to control your temper. Or you have difficulty resisting gossip, both in receiving and dispensing modes. Often you seem to go along with the crowd rather than living out your convictions. Your prayer life is erratic.

Not to worry. Like that ten-year-old prospective model, you are wanted as you are. God doesn't need you to put on new clothes or get your hair done. Instead, as the words of the nineteenth century hymn have it,

111

Gordon S. Jackson

God seeks you "Just as I am, without one plea, but that thy love was shed for me." No need to make changes, in appearance or in your heart; come as you are.

Note for example who gets invited in Jesus' parable of the man throwing a banquet. After the initial invitees come up with lame, even insulting, excuses why they will no longer come to this undoubtedly lavish meal, we read: "The servant came back and reported this to his master. Then the owner of the house became angry and ordered his servant, 'Go out quickly into the streets and alleys of the town and bring in the poor, the crippled, the blind and the lame.'"(Lk. 14:21) Notice that it's the poor, the crippled, the blind and the lame who are invited — the outcasts, shabbily dressed and utterly unable to raise their standing in life. You don't need to get into a certain tax bracket, get out of your wheelchair, or have cataract surgery so you can see properly and get around on your own.

You have been summoned. There is now neither the need nor the time to get your act together; from God's perspective, you're ready just as you are.

74: The Perfect Instrument

For we are God's handiwork, created in Christ Jesus to devote ourselves to the good deeds for which God has designed us.
— Ephesians 2:10, New English Bible

St. Ignatius of Loyola (1491-1556) was a Spanish priest who founded the Jesuit movement, famous for its missionary and educational work. The Jesuits played an important part in the Catholic counter-reformation. Included in Ignatius' legacy is a Latin phrase worthy of our attention. He described his ideal Jesuit as an *instrumentum conjunctum cum Deo,* "an instrument shaped to the hand of God." In other words, someone who was "a perfect fit" for God's hand.

It would be presumptuous for any one of us to think we've matured spiritually to the point where we're a perfect tool in the hand of God. Like Ignatius, however, we do well to see this as an ideal standard to attain, submitting ourselves to God's shaping and refining as we steadily work toward perfection as a tool in the Lord's work.

What remains in your life as a barrier to that perfect fit? What does God still need to do in your life to shape the tool that you are? To be sure, you're already of great use in Kingdom work. But what rough edges need smoothing out to improve God's grip? Or what needs sharpening so that you can better do the cutting God needs? Take a moment to reflect on what's needed for you to become the optimal *instrumentum conjunctum cum Deo.*

113

75: The Pilot Light

Suddenly a sound like the blowing of a violent wind came from heaven and filled the whole house where they were sitting. They saw what seemed to be tongues of fire that separated and came to rest on each of them. All of them were filled with the Holy Spirit and began to speak in other tongues as the Spirit enabled them.

— Acts 2:2-4

If your home is heated with gas, you may well have a pilot light for your water heater and furnace, and perhaps a gas stove. These pilot lights tell you the appliance is connected to its energy source and is ready for action. Something like the role of the Holy Spirit in a Christian's life, perhaps. Like that pilot light, the Spirit is always "on," as it were—unobtrusively in the background but always ready to fulfill its potential use.

Of all the analogies in this book, this one is perhaps most subject to criticism, as it may be seen as trivializing the person and role of the Holy Spirit. The point of the analogy, though, is to see a simple parallel that will help us better understand the character of the Holy Spirit.

Protestants in particular differ in our theology about the Holy Spirit, and how this third person of the Trinity enters our lives. Some of us believe that the Spirit automatically enters the Christian's life when he or she makes a commitment to Christ, whether or not we are baptized with water. Others believe instead that the Spirit comes upon us at baptism, even as infants. Then there's the issue described in Acts 19, where Paul encounters some believers who know nothing of the Holy Spirit, having been baptized only with the "baptism of John." They are described as believers, yet haven't been baptized, a lack that Paul immediately addresses: "When Paul placed his hands on them, the Holy Spirit came on them, and they spoke in tongues and prophesied."(Acts 19:6)

Which leads us to another question: Does baptism in the Spirit necessarily lead to speaking in tongues, and if it doesn't, is a second baptism then required?

We could dig deeper into the theological disputes that Christians have waged over the centuries regarding the exact nature of baptism and the Holy Spirit. For now, though, let us return to our image of the pilot light. Regardless of your theology, know that the divine equivalent of a pilot light is constantly burning in your life, ready to burst into full flame at a moment's notice.

76: Post-Production

... he who began a good work in you will carry it on to completion until the day of Christ Jesus.

— Philippians 1:6

Movie makers spend enormous amounts of money hiring actors and crew, preparing to shoot the film, perhaps flying everyone to exotic locations, and then doing the filming. But even when the last scenes have been shot, the movie is nowhere close to being done. Next comes post-production. This is when the laborious task of editing takes place, as well as blending the soundtrack and the musical score. Computer-generated imagery may also be needed.

So too with you and me, once we've committed our lives to Christ. In theological terms, regeneration has occurred; a new "work" has been created, like the raw footage in the film-making process. But there's a next step in our Christian lives, as the writer of Hebrews indicates: "...let us go on to perfection." (Heb. 6:1, *King James Version*)

That step is sanctification, as God continues to work on us, bringing us to that perfection. In other words, we're in post-production, where God needs to polish, refine, discipline, cut and add. As with movie making, it's a time-consuming business.

Paul says of God's work in our lives that "he who began a good work in you will carry it on to completion until the day of Christ Jesus." (Phil. 1:6) And when He *is* finished with all of us, it's going to be an astonishing show.

77: Professor Bigelow's Question

He who was seated on the throne said, "I am making everything new!" Then he said, "Write this down, for these words are trustworthy and true."
— Revelation 21:5

Henry Bigelow was a professor of medicine at Harvard University during the tenure of President Charles Eliot, a leader of legendary effectiveness during the mid-1800s. Bigelow was unhappy with the changes Eliot was proposing. "'How was it,' Bigelow asked one evening, 'that this faculty has gone on for eighty years managing its own affairs and doing it well — and now, within three or four months, it is proposed to change all our modes of carrying on the school?' Eliot's bland reply has been immortalized in academic lore: 'I can answer Dr. Bigelow's question very easily: There is a new President.'"[66]

The university was under new management, as it were, and under Eliot's leadership far-reaching changes were in the works. There's something striking about his quiet authority in his response to Dr. Bigelow. He is in effect saying, "I'm in charge here; I know what I'm doing. Deal with it."

So too with us when we turn our lives over to God. We have voluntarily placed ourselves under God's leadership and direction. He may well desire what we fear will be painful change in our lives. Yet we need to accept that like President Eliot, God is telling us, "I'm in charge here; I know what I'm doing. Deal with it."

---

[66] Hugh Hawkins, *Between Harvard and America.*

78: Radar, String Theory and Omniscience

Where were you when I laid the earth's foundation?
Tell me, if you understand.
Who marked off its dimensions? Surely you know!
Who stretched a measuring line across it? On what were its footings set,
or who laid its cornerstone —
while the morning stars sang together
and all the angels shouted for joy?

— Job 38:4-7

How is radar like the concept of string theory in physics? The answer requires that we step back to the middle of last century, when J. B. Phillips, an English pastor, writer, and translator of the New Testament into modern English, wrote a gem of a book called *Your God is Too Small*. He described various misconceptions people had of God, which invariably entailed people having an inadequate view of God's character and power. He described one such view, in which people saw God as a "grand old man," who had done good things in the past but who was out of touch with our complex contemporary world. Phillips cited a survey in which a group of teens were asked if they thought God could understand radar, then a relatively new technology that had emerged during World War II. Most of them answered "no," followed by a chuckle as they realized the absurdity of their answer.

Fast forward to today. What is your initial response to an updated question: Do you think God understands string theory? First, a definition, from Wikipedia: "In physics, string theory is a theoretical framework in which the point-like particles of particle physics are replaced by one-dimensional objects called strings. String theory describes how these strings propagate through space and interact with each other."[67] Another site focusing on physics adds, "String theory also requires six or seven extra dimensions of space, and it contains ways of relating large extra dimensions to small ones."[68] I began to get lost at the "point-like particles"

---

[67] https://en.wikipedia.org/wiki/String_theory#:~:text=In%20physics%2C%20string%20theory%20is,and%20interact%20with%20each%20other. Accessed Sept 4, 2023.

[68]
https://www.mathematicsmagazine.com/Articles/String_Theory.php#:~:text=

bit and gave up completely with those "six or seven extra dimensions of space."

Now I'm wondering if God is on top of this stuff. I conclude that if He isn't, and He's hit the limits of what is supposedly His omniscience, then we're back to the title of Phillips' book—and a conclusion that maybe my God *is* too small. Perhaps God is, after all, an outdated old fellow, with His flowing white beard, increasingly out of touch with a world of bitcoin and cloud computing, string theory and quantum physics.

On the other hand, those mid-twentieth century teens who knew to chuckle after their absurd answers about God and radar should also have us chuckling nervously at our effrontery in limiting the One who created everything, even those "point-like particles" and however many extra dimensions of space that He pleased.

String%20theory%20also%20requires%20six,the%20number%20of%20elementary%20particles. Accessed Sept. 4,2023.

79: Rainbows

And God said, "This is the sign of the covenant I am making between me and you and every living creature with you, a covenant for all generations to come: I have set my rainbow in the clouds, and it will be the sign of the covenant between me and the earth."

— Genesis 9:12-13

~~~~

A rainbow that shone like an emerald encircled the throne.

— Revelation 4:3

Throughout the world, in a wide range of traditional societies and religions, rainbows occupy a special place. Jean Chevalier and Alain Gheerbrant say they are seen as "both intermediaries and pathways between Heaven and Earth. They are the bridges used by gods and heroes when they travel between this Earth and the Other world."[69] They add, for example, that "Central African Pygmies believe that God uses the rainbow to show what He wishes to communicate with them," and that in ancient Greece, it was "a symbol of the relationship between Heaven and Earth and gods and mortals — a form of divine speech." Generally, say Chevalier and Gheerbrant, rainbows are seen positively, as "heralds of good things to come," and are "linked to the cycle of rebirth."

With a natural symbol this powerful, positive, and widespread, it would be curious if rainbows *did not* feature in Scripture. In the Judeo-Christian worldview, however, the rainbow goes beyond the kind of symbolism found in other societies. Yes, the Genesis 9 account includes elements of God communicating with humankind, as well as rebirth. But it goes further: The rainbow, God explicitly says, introduces a *covenantal* relationship. Here, God's divine speech initiates this new chapter of His relationship with humanity. The rainbow is not some kind of up- and down-escalator to heaven and back. It is presented clearly as a visible symbol or seal, like a wedding ring. In and of themselves, rainbows or wedding rings are only physical phenomena. It is what they *represent* that matters. The poet Robert Southey had it right when he began his sonnet, "To the Evening Rainbow," with the words, "Mild arch of promise." So did the more contemporary unidentified author who described a rainbow as "Heaven's promise in Technicolor."

Rainbows have other positive connotations in Scripture. For

---

[69] Jean Chevalier and Alain Gheerbrant, *A Dictionary of Symbols.*

example, we see God's glory and majesty in Ezekiel's experience: "Like the appearance of a rainbow in the clouds on a rainy day, so was the radiance around Him. This was the appearance of the likeness of the glory of the Lord. When I saw it, I fell facedown, and I heard the voice of one speaking." (Ez. 1:28)

Seeing that Genesis 1 and the book of Revelation are steeped in references to light, we should not be surprised to find that the rainbow soon appears in Genesis explicitly as a covenantal symbol, or that it makes a reprise appearance in John's vision of heaven. In a majestic passage in Revelation 4, John tries to capture in human language the indescribable glories of heaven. Having seen God seated in majesty, he adds, "A rainbow that shone like an emerald encircled the throne." (Rev. 4:3)

What better herald, to return to Chevalier and Gheerbrant's comment, could there be of "good things to come"?

80: The Rear-View Mirror

Remember that you were slaves in Egypt and that the LORD your God brought you out of there with a mighty hand and an outstretched arm.
— Deuteronomy 5:15

We ought always to be focused on the road ahead, on what lies ahead in our earthly journey. Nevertheless, any good driver would also keep an eye on the rear-view mirror. We need to ask, "Is anything happening behind us that we need to be aware of as we move forward?"

The Bible provides repeated instructions to do exactly that, in the form of a one-word instruction: *Remember*. The word appears 231 times in the *New International Version*, thus underscoring the importance of recognizing what we've learned on the journey so far, and to assure ourselves of the goodness of God that we've encountered over and over again.

Recalling what we have learned is only part one, however; the clear assumption is that we'll act in response to what we've remembered. Our driving forward is to be shaped by what we remember.

A pastor once said that in times of crisis, when you don't know where else to turn, look back to the basics of your faith and seek assurance from what you know to be true. Just as the children of Israel were told repeatedly to remember what God had done for them, so too should we. That "rear-view mirror of faith" is there for a reason.

81: Red Light, Green Light

For the foolishness of God is wiser than human wisdom, and the weakness of God is stronger than human strength.

— 1 Corinthians 1:25

~~~~~

A fellow is driving with his friend who goes straight through a red light, without even slowing. He decides his friend must not have noticed the signal. But a minute later, the driver does exactly the same at the next light. This is too much for the passenger and he says, "Do you realize you've gone straight through two red lights?"

"Yeah," the driver replies. "I always drive like that."

"Why?" says the friend.

"My brother taught me to drive that way," he explains, as he approaches a green light — and comes to a complete stop.

"What are you doing?" asks the passenger.

The driver responds, "Well, my brother could be coming the other way."

The driver is perfectly logical in his behavior — and perfectly wrong. Just like those folks who thought the earth was flat and that the sun circled around it. Or those top doctors in England in the 1800s who ridiculed Dr. Joseph Lister for his insistence that infections were caused by germs.

Or what of those many Christians who accepted Archbishop James Ussher's calculation that the world was created around 6 p.m. on October 22, 4004 BC?

In each case, the establishment of the day refused to accept scientific evidence. In other instances, Christians have embraced theological views that we have now discarded with embarrassment or even shame: notions on slavery, for example, or offering a biblical justification for the apartheid system of racial segregation in South Africa.

The antidote to these kinds of error? A healthy supply of humility and a readiness to begin contentious discussions by saying, "I could be wrong, but...." Checking your assumptions and listening to those with whom you disagree might just save you or your church the equivalent of a car crash.

82: Representing His Majesty

We are therefore Christ's ambassadors...

— 2 Corinthians 5:20

The year was 1777. Frederick the Great, the King of Prussia who had his quirky moments, had delighted in appointing as his ambassador to London a notoriously disreputable man. His purpose was clearly to indicate his contempt for the British government. Enter Hugh Elliot, the British diplomat assigned in turn by the British government to represent his country in Frederick's court. On arriving in Berlin, he presented himself to Frederick, who "mockingly asked Elliot what he thought of the Prussian envoy. 'Worthy to represent your majesty,' replied Elliot suavely."[70]

The British official's delightfully ambiguous response pointed to a powerful truth about Frederick's appointment: Any ambassador represents the character, for better or worse, of the one who has sent him. That is why ambassadors realize whatever other roles they may have, that of "representative" is paramount.

Do these representatives in some way convey a less than satisfactory impression of the government they represent? For whether ambassadors are good, bad, or indifferent, they clearly bear the stamp of the head of state who sent them.

As Christians, we too are a people sent forth. Over the centuries, Christians have been scattered around the globe, to serve as our Lord's emissaries as we represent Him and take the gospel message "to all nations."

Over the past two millennia, Christians have made massive and enduring contributions where they have lived out their lives and witness, both as individuals and through the church and other Christian organizations. It is no coincidence that most hospitals and private colleges in the United States were founded by Christians. It is no coincidence that individual Christians were involved in the abolitionist movement, in Britain and the United States, or in the US Civil Rights movement. One cannot begin to catalog the positive accomplishments and powerful witness that "Christ's ambassadors" have made in the places to which He has posted them during the history of the church.

---

[70] This story is recounted in *The Little Brown Book of Anecdotes*, ed. Clifton Fadiman.

But there is another side of the ledger. At times we have brought dishonor to God's name rather than honor. We have been poor ambassadors when we have proclaimed less than the full gospel of Christ crucified. We have been poor ambassadors when we have proclaimed the "gospel plus" — the gospel *plus* a certain cultural package or political ideology, or the gospel *plus* a certain worship style.

We have been poor ambassadors when, instead of letting a watching world "know we are Christians by our love, by our love," we present a church marked by hundreds of denominations and other divisions, a body that hardly shows "We are one in the spirit." Whether one looks at the Crusades or the Inquisition, the church's checkered record on slavery or race relations, or the tangled ties of Western colonialism with mission efforts to South America, Africa or Asia, the church has much in its history we Christians wish was not there.

An important difference between ambassadors representing their home countries and Christians representing God is that we are forever stumbling and falling short of His expectations of us. Even as believers, we are still drawn to sinful conduct, as Paul writes in Romans of himself: "I cannot understand my own behavior. I fail to carry out the things I want to do, and I find myself doing the very things I hate." (Rom. 7:15, *Jerusalem Bible*)

In our prayers of confession to God, that is exactly what we should bring before Him: our sense of woeful inadequacy to serve as His ambassadors. Yet, in His marvelous grace, God says in reply, "You are forgiven. Don't worry about whatever damage you have done. Right the wrongs you need to and fix what you can, and I will take care of the rest. My Kingdom is far more resilient than you know; I can handle even the worst of your blunders and harm to My reputation. Now let's get back to the task at hand."

As ambassadors for the King of Heaven, we need never fear being recalled from our posts because we "blew it." No, it is another of God's astonishing acts of grace that He keeps working with us, with infinite patience, so long as we seek to honor Him where we have been assigned — and as we continue to depend on the Holy Spirit so that we might become worthy of our ambassadorial calling.

83: Ripeness

I tell you, open your eyes and look at the fields! They are ripe for harvest.
— John 4:35

I was studying Spanish in Guatemala in 1992, during yet another season of political instability in that country's seemingly perpetual struggle for democratic rule. One of my teachers, eager for a more just social order, said that the climate wasn't yet ripe enough for change. Things were still "too green," as he put it. Sadly, three decades on, that beautiful but beleaguered country still hasn't attained the stability of which my teacher dreamed. Perhaps conditions remain "too green."

What about us? Are there areas in our lives that resist ripening to bear the fruit that God expects of us? When we reflect on Paul's list — "[T]he fruit of the Spirit is love, joy, peace, forbearance, kindness, goodness, faithfulness, gentleness and self-control..." (Gal. 5:22) — how do we rate?

And what about others whose lives we seek to influence, either mentoring them in their faith or aspiring to introduce them to the saving knowledge of the gospel? James S. Stewart, a Scottish pastor and author, said that pastors should remind themselves of the opportunity facing them each Sunday morning: "God is to be in action today, through me, for these people; this day may be crucial, this service decisive, for someone now ripe for the vision of Jesus."[71]

The concept of "ripeness," then, calls for our alertness to conditions that ripen the spiritual fruit we are already equipped to produce. What "spiritual greenhouse" conditions would encourage that process?

---

[71] Quoted in J. Doberstein: *Minister's Prayer Book.*

84: The Rosetta Stone

Then Jesus told him, "Because you have seen me, you have believed; blessed are those who have not seen and yet have believed."

— John 20:29

The Rosetta Stone was vitally important in deciphering ancient Egyptian hieroglyphs, a system of writing previously unintelligible to scholars. But the stone, discovered in 1799, ultimately proved to be breakthrough for one reason: the same message was written in three languages on the surviving piece of stone, one of those being Greek. Ingenious work by French and British translators led to the unraveling of a message that had been buried for about 2,000 years, and a leap forward in Egyptology. The stone, about the size of a coffee table, is now on display in the British Museum.

The term "Rosetta Stone" has entered everyday conversation as a symbol for anything that "gives a clue to understanding," according to the *Merriam-Webster's Dictionary* definition. A Rosetta Stone is the key that solves a mystery or makes everything clear. And it's that kind of clarity C.S. Lewis referred to when he said: "I believe in Christianity as I believe in the sun—not only because I see it, but because by it I see everything else."[72] Like Lewis, for some people their commitment to Christ comes only after a long time grappling with reality. Matters of faith don't make sense. No matter how sincere one might be, all the talk about God, Jesus, the Bible, the church and Jesus' followers simply doesn't line up. Then one day, somehow everything lines up: the key fits, the cryptic language is decoded. There's an "aha!" moment of stunning magnitude as the Holy Spirit breaks through to someone's heart and suddenly the sunlight makes clear everything that has been there all along. Now, like Lewis, the person says, "I believe."

---

[72] Quoted in Gordon S. Jackson: *Quotes for the Journey, Wisdom for the Way.*

85: Rudderless

I will instruct you and teach you in the way you should go; I will counsel you with My loving eye on you.

— *Psalm 32:8*

~~~~~

Shirley Toulson, in her book The Celtic Year, *says: "They [Celtic pilgrims] were emulating Abraham, who left his settled homeland at the command of Yahweh, and like him they made no plans but trusted that God would direct their footsteps. We are told that they even went to sea rudderless, letting the currents, the tides, and the winds take them to a destination known only to God."*

Compare that commitment to "rudderless-ness" to Noah's adventure in the ark. He too drifted rudderless, afloat for nearly a year before he arrived at his God-ordained destination on Mount Ararat.

We humans, however, are not excited about the idea of being rudderless. Living as we do in an era of GPS directions, we depend on our smartphones to tell us to turn left in one hundred yards or that "Your destination is on your right." The idea of beginning a journey without our phone would make many of us uncomfortable; doing so without even having a destination in mind is unthinkable.

Yet there are times in our lives when God may ask exactly that: to set out, with Him, on a journey with no clear destination. "Leave your phone behind," He says. "Don't worry about the lack of a rudder. I know where We're going. Trust Me."

~~~~~

I know I cannot drift
Beyond his love and care.

— *John Greenleaf Whittier*[73]

---

[73] From his poem "The Eternal Goodness."

86: A Sense of Occasion — A Satire

Yours, LORD, is the greatness and the power, and the glory and the majesty and the splendor....

— 1 Chronicles 29:11

~~~~~

When Lucy, in C. S. Lewis' "The Lion, the Witch and the Wardrobe" learns about Aslan the lion, she asks if he is safe. Mr. Beaver responds, "Safe? Who said anything about safe? 'Course he isn't safe. But he's good. He's the King, I tell you."

Some rules on meeting His Majesty, King Charles III of the United Kingdom of Great Britain and Northern Ireland:
- Stand when he enters the room.
- Shake his hand only if he offers his to you first; shake it gently and do not pump it.
- Citizens of the United Kingdom or Commonwealth countries should bow gently on meeting him (men) or curtsey (women).
- Do not otherwise touch him, by hugging, putting your arm around him, and so on. Do not engage in other unexpected behaviors.
- Cell phone protocol: under no circumstances let your phone ring. Given the occasion, that is utterly inappropriate. You are, after all, in the presence of royalty.

Some rules for attending our church on Sunday:
- Come dressed as you are; we are a friendly church and want you to feel comfortable, so tank tops, shorts and flip-flops are fine.
- If you run a little late, don't worry about it; you're still most welcome.
- It's okay to bring your cup of Starbucks into worship. Donuts or other munchies are fine too.
- Getting up to take a restroom break is fine.
- Cell phone protocol: it's okay to text or check e-mails, but under no circumstances let your phone ring. Given the occasion, that is utterly inappropriate. You are, after all, in the presence of royalty.

87: A Sick Joke

And my God will meet all your needs according to the riches of His glory in Christ Jesus.

— Philippians 4:19

You're driving through a remote part of the country when you realize your rental car's gas tank seems smaller than you assumed. Your need for a gas station becomes more and more urgent. Your young son and daughter are asleep in the back. It would be one thing to be stranded on your own in the middle of nowhere, but you don't want to think about having them being stranded with you, as it starts getting dark.

You pray more fervently for a gas station. The orange light warning you that you're low on gas comes on. Your prayers intensify. Then, as dusk is falling you see in the distance a small community and, praise be, a gas station — with its lights still on.

"Thank You, Lord," you mutter, as your daughter begins to stir on the back seat. You pull up at the pump, only to see a sign crudely written on a piece of cardboard, "Diesel only — out of gas."

"No!," you say aloud, fully awakening both kids. Then, to yourself, you say, "What is this, Lord, some kind of sick joke?"

~~~~~

As the children of Israel found at the place they appropriately named "Marah" — or bitterness — we sometimes have to deal with a God Who responds to desert-level thirst by giving us undrinkable, bitter water. What sort of God *is* this? It appears that He's a God Who is all too aware of our partial reliance on Him — and then demands more. We come to God in our desperation and beg His help, which He generously gives us in the form of water in the desert or a gas station in the boonies. At that point, we revert to our independence, and in effect say, "Thanks, we'll take it from here."

He in turn says, "Hmmm... Still too much self-reliance there. Let's notch this up a bit." Then He reminds us that He is Lord over *everything*, including water quality and gas shortages. "Be careful not to presume on My grace," He tells us. "Don't forget that the groceries you plan to buy today are on the shelves by My grace. Or that you got to work today without a serious car accident; yep, also by My grace."

~~~~~

You approach the gas station attendant, who appears to be closing for the night. "Don't you have even a few gallons of regular, somewhere?

I've got my kids in the car and I'm really low...." You make your plea, hoping you're not sounding as pathetic as you feel.

"Lemme see," he says. But instead of checking his supplies he goes to the back of your rental car. "Just as I thought," he says, having perused those silvery letters indicating the model.

"You're driving a diesel." [74]

---

[74] This story is for my son Matthew and his wife, Ella. They will understand.

88: A Software Update

For we do not have a high priest who is unable to empathize with our weaknesses, but we have one who has been tempted in every way, just as we are.
— 1 Corinthians 10:13

Remember the message your computer sends you when it is updating? Things like "Do not switch off until this is complete" and "This may take some time" and "You may use other programs while it is updating."

Sort of like God needing to do some stretching in your life. "This may take some time," for example. Nor are you to check out of normal activities while the stretching is occurring. Nor do you know how you might be different when the update is finished.

There's a difference too between the announced updates and those things happening behind the scenes; always your computer security system is alert to threats and is quietly working in the background to protect you from viruses, malware, ransomware and other cybercrud. The Holy Spirit is filling a comparable role in your Christian walk. We know from Romans 8:26-27 that "...the Spirit helps us in our weakness. We do not know what we ought to pray for, but the Spirit himself intercedes for us through wordless groans. And he who searches our hearts knows the mind of the Spirit, because the Spirit intercedes for God's people in accordance with the will of God."

Given our free will we can sometimes override the protection that God affords us, knowingly making a sinful choice that's the equivalent of stupidly opening an e-mail that your McAfee or Norton software warns you look suspicious. But the message reads something like, "Hungry? Try this exquisite fruit of this all-new tree of the knowledge of good and evil, for a taste like you've never experienced before. Even better than Mom's cooking. Guaranteed fair trade and locally sourced."

Usually we're not so dumb as to respond to such temptation. But God knows our ever-changing circumstances and how the Tempter will vary his approach in attempting to break through our spiritual equivalent of a firewall. Whether we're aware or not of the divine protections built into our life, we can be sure that God never lets our spiritual software be inadequate to the challenges and temptations we will face.

("Hmmm... Even better than Mom's cooking, you say?")

89: Spiritual Aikido and Jubilant Adventure

But I tell you, do not resist an evil person. If anyone slaps you on the right cheek, turn to them the other cheek also. And if anyone wants to sue you and take your shirt, hand over your coat as well. If anyone forces you to go one mile, go with them two miles.

– Matthew 5:39-41

Aikido is a modern Japanese martial art with a difference. Developed in the first half of the twentieth century by Morihei Ueshiba, aikido was influenced by his philosophical and religious beliefs that led to an unusual emphasis. Practitioners of the art were trained not only to defend themselves, but to do so in a way that avoided injury to their attackers. Rather than disabling an attacker, aikido practitioners needed to focus on that person's welfare as well as their own.

If this approach sounds familiar to Christians, it should. Hint: think of Jesus instructing His disciples on spiritual aikido in dealing with their enemies:

> *But I tell you, do not resist an evil person. If anyone slaps you on the right cheek, turn to them the other cheek also. And if anyone wants to sue you and take your shirt, hand over your coat as well. If anyone forces you to go one mile, go with them two miles. Give to the one who asks you, and do not turn away from the one who wants to borrow from you. (Mt. 5:39-42)*

Just as twenty centuries later, a thoughtful martial arts instructor expressed concern for both the attacked and the attacker, so Jesus told us how to respond in love. And that is a key difference: in aikido, one is concerned to protect oneself while also being of a generous spirit in not injuring the attacker. Jesus, though, was instructing us in how to *love* our enemies, not just to neutralize them. We believe in a God Who can transform bad things into good, a God Who can make dead bones come alive.[75] As the New Zealand scholar E. M. Blaiklock said in commenting on Psalm 18, and David's gratitude for all God had given him, "If God was over all, permitting no suffering that he was not able to turn to usefulness, allowing no defeat which he was not certain to transmute into his own form of victory, then life was gladness, confidence, jubilant adventure."[76]

---

[75] Ezekiel 37.
[76] E. M. Blaiklock: *Handbook of Bible People.*

We Christians who are practicing spiritual aikido, then, ought not only be blessed with such gladness, confidence, and jubilant adventure, we should be drawing our attackers into joining us in such a state of being.

90: Spiritual Autism

Ask and you will receive, and your joy will be complete.

— John 16:24

The Autism Society defines this condition as "a complex, lifelong developmental disability that typically appears during early childhood and can impact a person's social skills, communication, relationships, and self-regulation. Autism is defined by a certain set of behaviors and is a 'spectrum condition' that affects people differently and to varying degrees."

Without diminishing the significance of this condition, and the difficulty it presents for parents, teachers and those coping with autism, the definition above provides a useful analogy for Christians. People with autism in various ways fall short of what we'd regard as normal or "ideal" behavior. And so do Christians.

Each of us has some area of our lives where, at least to some degree, we "don't get it" in the way other people might. For example, for some Christians worship music doesn't "click" for them; joining in song on Sunday morning means nothing. If anything, it may irritate them as they see how others are immersing themselves joyfully in the music while they're left cold. Others may struggle with prayer. Or perhaps it's Bible study and they get no spiritual food by digging into a passage of Scripture.

This analogy has one important limitation. Unlike autism itself, which the definition said is a lifelong disability, Christians can potentially change and grow, overcoming the "autism-like" features that serve as a spiritual disability. But whether they do or not, we need to be aware that we're all at some place on a spectrum that reflects our spiritual deficiencies. That calls for introspection into our own lives and identifying those areas where God still needs to shape and mold us. And we anticipate such change in full confidence that one day whatever doesn't "click" for us now in our Christian life will be irrelevant, and we'll know a new unblemished "normal" that we can only imagine.

91: The Sultan's Horse

Truly I tell you, if you have faith as small as a mustard seed, you can say to this mountain, "Move from here to there" and it will move. Nothing will be impossible for you.

— Matthew 17:20

A sultan with a perverse sense of humor would now and again present a challenge to the prisoners in his jail who were serving life sentences. He offered anyone his freedom if after one year he could teach the sultan's favorite horse to speak. If the would-be teacher failed, however, he would be executed.

Nobody took him up on this offer. That is, until one day Mustafa stepped up and accepted the challenge. As he was preparing to move to undertake his task, his fellow prisoners wanted to know why he was making such a foolhardy move.

"Three reasons," he said. "In the next year, the sultan may die. The horse may die. Or, who knows, the horse may learn to speak."

~~~~~

While Christians believe in miracles, most of us suspect things will not go well for Mustafa. Barring a miracle (or the death of the sultan or the horse), it's highly improbable this prisoner will gain his freedom. Christians seeking a miracle know that they serve a God Who, as Lynne Bundesen puts it, has not forgotten how to part the sea. Whether it's the Children of Israel's miraculous liberation from Egypt and their repeated experience of miracles in the desert, or the New Testament miracles of Jesus' incarnation and resurrection, Christians should never doubt God's capacity to transcend the laws of nature. For a God Who can resurrect Jesus from the dead, getting a horse to speak would be a breeze. (After all, we have the precedent of a talking donkey, in the surprisingly amusing Old Testament story of Balaam.)

There's one catch, however. Is the requested miracle in keeping with God's overall will and purposes? God, being God, could arrange for an orchestra of manatees to play Beethoven's Fifth if He wanted. But God isn't a show-off or a divine being doing magic tricks as a hobby. So when Jesus promises us that if we have faith, we can move mountains, He's assuming we're calling upon divine power for divine purposes — not for some frivolous end.

Nevertheless, miracles *do* sometimes happen, but that's according to God's agenda, not ours. And yes, we all love them when they occur, as

Mark Batterson says. However, he adds, "We just don't like being in a position that necessitates one."[77] Like Mustafa.

---

[77] Mark Batterson: *The Circle Maker.*

92: Switching Tanks

The righteous cry out, and the LORD *hears them; He delivers them from all their troubles.*

— *Psalm 34:17*

In his riveting book, *Shadow Divers*, Robert Kurson tells the story of some deep-sea divers who found an unidentified, sunken World War II German submarine off the New Jersey coast. Neither the US authorities nor the Germans had any record of this vessel.

Kurson describes the painstaking research that resolved the mystery of how the sub got where it did. As the story unfolds, Kurson describes the hazardous work conditions that professional divers routinely face. One of the worst scenarios a diver can encounter, other than getting trapped in wreckage, is to unexpectedly run low on an air tank. If that happened to us, our first inclination would be moderate to intense panic, and thus make our situation even worse.

Yet professional divers have disciplined themselves to avoid doing what is instinctual in every human: to breathe. Instead, these divers force themselves to transcend their instincts and the demands of biology, refusing to breathe while they cope with the crisis at hand.

Not breathe? Impossible. But for these seasoned individuals they know that panic is a worse alternative, as they expertly stop breathing while changing tanks.

God makes a different kind of demand of us, in effect one where we need comparable self-discipline. Recall when Jesus said: "If anyone slaps you on the right cheek, turn to them the other cheek also. And if anyone wants to sue you and take your shirt, hand over your coat as well. If anyone forces you to go one mile, go with them two miles."(Mt. 5:39-41)

Who of us is naturally disposed to responding to a literal slap in the face by keeping our cool, and turning to our assailant and in effect saying, "Look, here's another one—hit me here too if you want. But I'm not hitting you back." Or giving your coat in addition to the shirt demanded of you. Or telling that Roman soldier who has commandeered you to carry his pack a mile, "Oh, it's no problem; it's a gorgeous day and I'll gladly go another mile." That's not how we are expected to respond to an oppressor who had the authority to force us to go that grueling mile.

The Interpreter's Bible Commentary poses the question, "What does such teaching mean? Our imagination recoils before it, and our everyday morality... flatly contradicts it. Christ has in mind the injured man. Such a man's concern for justice is never pure: it is subtly entangled with vindictiveness. Christ warns him against that revenge."

Likewise, the *African Bible Commentary* echoes the need to avoid revenge when wronged. On the contrary, it says, "Christians are called upon to be generous even to those who appear to be their oppressors."

Yet because powerlessness may make revenge out of the question, we settle instead for hatred. While Jesus has told us to love our enemies, the desire for revenge is so ingrained in us that it will take a super-human effort to honor His command—and His example... With the help of the Holy Spirit we can respond as our Lord Himself did when facing the most excruciating pressure; never did He compromise Himself, but never did He lower Himself to the tactics of His accusers either.

Our moment of crisis may leave us in effect with the air in our own tank registering close to empty; we cannot carry on relying on our own supply. Time to hold our breath and do the impossible, while switching tanks to one filled by the Holy Spirit. We will be able to breathe in a way that will astonish those who have brought us harm, and lead them to say, "Who *are* these people?"

93: Tethered

No one can come to me unless the Father who sent Me draws them....
— John 6:44

~~~~~

  *A police officer on patrol noticed a young boy running the
perimeter of a high-rise apartment complex. The officer noticed the
boy was doing this again and again. Finally, intrigued, the officer
asked the boy what he was doing.*
  "I'm running away from home," he said.
  "But you're not going very far, are you?"
  "Well, my dad won't let me cross the street."

  The story illustrates three points about our relationship with God.
One is that at times we've had it up to here with God; if that's how you
treat your friends, we conclude, I'm running away from home.

  The second is that even though we've left home we somehow find we
can't go all that far. We keep running around the building, defiantly
showing God He can't treat us the way He did—yet at the same time
knowing we can't cross the street either. He still has a mysterious hold
over us; angry though we are, we remain tethered to our Father.

  Third, as we'd tell anyone who asked, we still have a home and still
have a Father, Whose rules we intuitively know we must obey. So,
notwithstanding our tantrum, we know not to stray too far.

  Sooner or later we'll calm down and head back inside. Dad will be
there, waiting, and He announces, as if we've never been gone, that dinner
will be another five minutes.

94: "Three Minutes..."

I consider my life worth nothing to me; my only aim is to finish the race and complete the task the Lord Jesus has given me....

— Acts 20:24

You may well know the name of Roger Bannister, the first man to run a sub-four-minute mile. You're less likely, though, to know the names of Chris Brasher and Chris Chataway. They were the fellow runners without whose help Bannister would almost certainly not have succeeded. They were his "pace men," who ran hard on the first laps to ensure Bannister was maintaining a pace that would average less than a minute a lap of the 440-yard track.

The quest had long eluded runners, but Bannister and other athletes were getting close. Then, on the evening of May 6, 1954, at a track outside Oxford, England, the young medical student made history. As the crowd of 3,000 wondered if this might be *the* race, the announcer teased them by dragging out the details: "Ladies and gentlemen, here is the result of event nine, the one mile: first, number forty one, R. G. Bannister, Amateur Athletic Association and formerly of Exeter and Merton Colleges, Oxford, with a time which is a new meeting and track record, and which — subject to ratification — will be a new English Native, British National, All-Comers, European, British Empire and World Record. The time was three..." At that point the crowd exploded in applause and didn't hear the rest: "...minutes and 59.4 seconds."

While international attention was showered on the young doctor-in-training from Oxford University, Brasher and Chataway were understandably much in the background. Two figures in the New Testament provide a parallel: Barnabas and Timothy. Barnabas appears in Acts thirty-three times. Whenever he appears with Paul, it's clear that Barnabas lets Paul take the lead. He's willing to be a support, more in the background. Never seeking glory for himself, he also champions the cause of John Mark, his cousin, after this younger man had a falling out with Paul. Barnabas is clearly well received and highly regarded by the young church, which recognizes him as the leader he is — but far less dominating a figure than Paul.

Then there's Timothy, of whom William Barclay writes, "Timothy's great value was that he was always willing to go anywhere... He is the patron saint of all those who are quite content with second place, so long as they can serve."[78] Like Barnabas, he accompanied Paul on his travels and Paul regarded him with special fondness, calling him his "true son in the faith." (1 Tim. 1:2) Also like Barnabas, he was more concerned to serve than seek first place.

These men fulfilled some of the roles that Chris Brasher and Chris Chataway did for Roger Bannister on that day in 1954. They were by his side, pushing him on to fulfill his role, and content with forsaking the spotlight. Barnabas and Timothy were of inestimable help in Paul's ministry and modeled for the rest of us 2,000 years later that second place is just fine.

[78] William Barclay: *The Daily Study Bible: Philippians, Colossians and Thessalonians.*

95: The Toddler

See what great love the Father has lavished on us, that we should be called children of God! And that is what we are.

– 1 John 3:1

Like a typical toddler, John Jr. loved to visit his dad's office. In particular, he enjoyed going to his favorite hiding place: under the splendid desk.

But this was no ordinary office. Nor was it an ordinary toddler. The eighteen-month-old was the son of President John Kennedy. And the Oval Office desk was likewise in a category of its own, made from the oak timbers of a former British naval vessel, the *HMS Resolute*, and given as a gift from Queen Victoria to President Rutherford B. Hayes in 1880.

Not many toddlers have the chance to play in such an august setting. Nor would a young child like John Jr. have the slightest idea of how privileged he was to be in this inner sanctum of presidential power. John Jr. couldn't begin to grasp the importance of this setting, the place where his father the President would preside over discussions and decisions of great moment.

John Jr. would typically be taken out during those high-powered meetings, blissfully unaware of the power his father wielded as the leader of the free world and the military might at his disposal. But what he could understand was his father's love, and that he was welcome (at least some of the time) in this special place in this big house.

It's a picture not lost on us, as our heavenly Father welcomes us into His inner sanctum, to play in His office, as it were, to find our equivalent of a hiding place under a desk. But more than any favorite spot in our Father's presence, we're assured of His infinite love and the unshakeable knowledge that we belong right there. Like John Jr., we have not even the tiniest grasp on what our heavenly Father is up to, the extent of His power, or the forces at His disposal. None of that matters to us.

Unlike John Jr., however, we are not about to be scooped up by the equivalent of a White House nanny and taken away for a diaper check or a nap. By sheer grace, we have been admitted to God's presence, as His children, and we are there to stay.

96: Unmasked

For now we see only a reflection as in a mirror; then we shall see face to face.
Now I know in part; then I shall know fully, even as I am fully known.
— 1 Corinthians 13:12

The ubiquitous presence of masks during COVID 19 had a range of consequences in addition to protecting us from the virus. Some people developed skin conditions from wearing their masks for lengthy periods. Others, who were hard of hearing, often struggled to understand what someone was saying, indicating just how reliant they had been on seeing people's lips forming their words. And only long-term research will reveal what impact mask wearing had on infants, who were deprived of seeing the full faces of their caregivers, and thus missing the visual cues that are crucial in their development.

Masks also ushered in those awkward moments in the supermarket, when you saw someone whom you thought you knew but couldn't be sure. The hair and top third of his visage led you to think, "That's Hyram, from church, isn't it?" But uncertainty reigned and you waited to see if the supposed Hyram recognized and acknowledged you. He may have been grappling with the same uncertainty. So, either you ignored each other; or you said hello and learned that, yes, your first impressions were accurate, followed by a pleasant chat; or you dealt with the mutual embarrassment of realizing that you were indeed strangers to each other. No Hyram.

Paul speaks to this phenomenon of partial recognition in his famous chapter on love: "For now we see only a reflection as in a mirror; then we shall see face to face. Now I know in part; then I shall know fully, even as I am fully known." (1 Cor. 13:12) In our present state, we live with an incomplete understanding of God and His plans and purposes. We cannot see His face, not because He is masked but because of our human limitations. As we've noted elsewhere[79] even Moses was not permitted to see God face to face, which would have led to his death.

We wear masks for two main reasons: to protect our health, as you and millions of others did during COVID (and perhaps you still are in public out of caution), or to deliberately hide your identity (think bank robbers or masked balls). But health concerns will be irrelevant for our new, resurrection bodies. Likewise, we can be highly confident that none of heaven's inhabitants will need to mask up for occasions like bank

---

[79] See **"As It Were" — A Speculation.**

robberies.

As far as we know, then, there'll be no need, either protective or sinister, to wear a mask. We can't be too sure about those masked balls, though.

97: Wasted Armor

Therefore put on the full armor of God, so that when the day of evil comes, you may be able to stand your ground...

— Ephesians 6: 13

If you read the rest of Paul's analogy about the armor God provides us, you'll see how comprehensive it is—at least, for protecting our front. We have a belt, breastplate, helmet, shield, and sword. But nothing for our back. God's people are not expected to, or equipped for, retreat from the battle. God prepares us only for marching toward the enemy.

What He provides for our protection, though, is only part of the story. Assuming you're comfortable with Paul's military image (and some people are not), two other considerations affect our fighting role. One is our need to be prepared for battle on that "day of evil" that he predicts will come. We need to be fighting fit; a suit of armor is little help to an untrained, unprepared soldier. That means we are to work at our "spiritual fitness," grounded in an always-growing grasp of Scripture and in prayer.

The other consideration is that of duty: We are to show up on the day of battle. We do not have the luxury of avoiding the spiritual battles that will inevitably lie ahead. Jesus promised us hardship, telling His disciples they needed to take up their cross. Peter too spoke of the trials that would accompany the Christian life: "... for a little while you may have had to suffer grief in all kinds of trials." (1 Pet. 1:6)

Turning to run isn't a wise move; God may "have your back," but that suit of armor isn't much help for the fleeing soldier.

98: Where, Indeed?

And Noah and his sons and his wife and his sons' wives entered the ark to escape the waters of the flood.

— Genesis 7:7

Wisława Szymborska, a Polish poet and winner of the Nobel Prize for literature, began one of her poems by asking, "An endless rain is just beginning. Into the Ark, for where else can you go."[80] Where, indeed?

Most of the time our lives go along routinely, following a daily, weekly, monthly and even annual rhythm. We get lulled into a false sense of security and forget that we live in a perpetual state of vulnerability. Then, every so often, something breaks through to remind us how fragile we humans are: a tsunami or earthquake, a devastating drought, a major war that claims millions of lives, or COVID-19. At such moments, where do we turn for help? With the COVID-19 pandemic, most of us turned to science to protect us. Or in other times of international crisis, maybe we want our leaders to resort to military power. At an individual level, we may be tempted to seek safety and security in our bank balance, our career, our relationships, or our independence.

For Christians, our only sure sanctuary is God Himself. As the endless rain begins, we know our ultimate salvation rests in the Ark. Of course, "the Ark" is not a panacea for all human ills. No doubt many Christians were among the millions around the world who died in the COVID-19 pandemic.

Instead, Christians seek the Ark as a symbol of God's sanctuary and protection for our souls, if not our bodies. While we're entitled to pray for sunshine to mark our days, we know that when an endless rain seems to have begun, we need not fear; God has an Ark in readiness for us.

---

[80] From her poem, "Into the Ark," in *View with a Grain of Sand*.

99: White Noise

Peace I leave with you; my peace I give you. I do not give to you as the world gives. Do not let your hearts be troubled and do not be afraid.

— John 14:27

Some of us who have difficulty sleeping resort to a machine that will generate white noise. It is intriguing to read the science underlying how white noise can help you drop off into dreamland and stay there. But the key point for us is that for some people, white noise is a great boon.

The reason, says Seth Horowitz, a neuroscientist, is that "hearing still works while you're asleep."[81] Because we cannot help "listening" to what's going on around us when we sleep, we may wake when, for example, a neighbor's dog unexpectedly barks at 3 a.m. One website describing white noise notes that it's not the sudden noise per se that wakes you, it is "the sudden change or inconsistencies in noise that jar you" into wakefulness. What the white noise does is to block out those changes or inconsistencies for a light sleeper.

There are times in the Christian life when we too may be struggling to find a sense of peace or calm. We may be suffering from a health crisis or have lost a loved one unexpectedly. Whatever our situation, we feel far removed from the state that Jesus promised His followers: "I have come that they may have life, and have it to the full." (Jn. 10:10) Instead, we're in survival mode—barely.

Now is the time we need divine soothing, God's tender embrace while we need time to heal. We need Him to shut out everything else, everything that would disturb our time of rest and recovery. "Lord, please shut out the chatter and the barking dogs," we pray. And He answers our prayer with His equivalent of white noise, cocooning us with the soothing sound of His presence that blocks out those unwanted noises. We enjoy the restoration we so urgently need.

But we need to know the white noise is only for the night. Come tomorrow, we will awake. The healing is accomplished and we are rested. We are ready, as it were, to re-enter the game. And we put the white noise machine away until it's needed once more.

---

[81] https://www.soundofsleep.com/sleep-central-the-benefits-of-sleep-therapy-systems/#:~:text=White%20noise%20creates%20a%20masking,How%20Hearing%20%20Shapes%20the%20Mind. Accessed Sept. 4, 2023.

100: Wrong Exit

For the Son of Man came to seek and to save the lost.

— Luke 19:10

You really blew it this time. On that straight and narrow road that God has set before you, you didn't just let your attention wander and drift toward the road's shoulder, where the sound of tires on the rumble strip gave you a frightening warning that you were close to trouble. That time, you corrected the steering in a moment, averting the danger of a wreck. You recall how shaken you were, grateful for that safety measure, and all was well.

Instead, this time was far worse. You weren't just negligent; you willfully chose a tempting looking exit and left that straight and narrow road completely. For whatever reason, you yielded to temptation on a biggie: you embezzled funds from work/the PTA/your church; you committed adultery; you hit a cyclist while driving home from work and, panic stricken, drove off; you got drunk and seriously hurt your four-year-old when he wouldn't stop whining. Or whatever. The point is, it's a big enough transgression against God, and those you've betrayed, to leave you drowning in guilt and convinced that God no longer wants anything to do with you. You can't envision any way of getting back on that straight and narrow road.

It's precisely at that point, where you find yourself close to despair, that God miraculously provides out of nowhere an on-ramp back onto that road you foolishly exited. God is the consummate road engineer. Regardless of the terrain, He's able instantly to pave the way for us to get back on track with Him.

We can picture Jesus scouring the landscape for any who've taken a wrong exit. "For the Son of Man came to seek and to save the lost." (Lk. 19:10) Whether we choose to use the new on-ramp created especially for us is another matter. Tragically, some who've strayed from God's highway opt never to return, even though like the father in the story of the Prodigal Son, God is always hoping, waiting for us to "come home."

There are probably others with whom we also need to reconcile, others who were hurt by our actions, and possibly legal issues to face. But the emphasis here is on what we fear is a shattered relationship with God because of what we've done, something so egregious or life-changing that we fear we can never restore our relationship with Him. Philip Yancey

148

offers a word of reassurance: "Grace means there is nothing we can do to make God love us more... and there is nothing we can do to make God love us less."[82]

The on-ramp is always open.

---

[82] Philip Yancey: *What's So Amazing About Grace*.

101: Your Photo on God's Fridge Door

But the very hairs on your heads are all counted. Away with fear: you are more precious than a multitude of sparrows.

— Luke 12:7, Weymouth New Testament

It's probably true to say that no two fridges have exactly the same contents. The mix of meat and veggies, fruit and bottles of salad dressings, butter and eggs, and whatever else, in whatever quantities, in your fridge is probably unique. And if you decorate the outside of your fridge, the same applies there. Photos of family members, Compassion International or World Vision children whom you support, a friend in the Jesuit Volunteers Corps, crayon drawings by your five-year-old son or granddaughter — once again a unique combination.

Then there's God's fridge door. (It's not clear why God needs a fridge; nothing can spoil in heaven. But trust me, it's a large one, with an ice maker and water dispenser — top of the line.) And on the door is your picture. It's there, God tells you, because you're much loved, just like those children or grandchildren whose photos adorn your fridge. God cares about you and is always mindful of you, just like your missionary families' pics.

Naturally, your photo on God's fridge isn't the only one; it's in good company. You marvel that God can somehow keep track of all of them. Then again, He *is* God. But the even greater marvel perhaps is that God has placed *your* picture on the fridge in the first place.

ABOUT THE AUTHOR

Gordon S. Jackson is a South African-born educator and author. He grew up in Cape Town, where he received his undergraduate education. He then completed an MA at Wheaton College in Illinois and worked as a reporter and editor for a newsmagazine in Johannesburg.

Returning to the United States, he then completed his doctorate in mass communication at Indiana University in 1983. He then began his teaching career at Whitworth University, a liberal arts institution in Spokane, WA. He retired in 2015 but has remained active as an author.

Your Photo on God's Fridge Door is his nineteenth book. In addition to two scholarly books, he has written three satirical novels, an anthology of satirical pieces about the church, and several other faith-related books.

He is married to another South African, who helps to keep his accent honest. He and his wife have two adult children and identical twin granddaughters, who have been officially certified as the cutest, brightest, and most engaging grandchildren in the continental USA.

THANK YOU!

Thank you for reading this book from Mt. Zion Ridge Press.

If you enjoyed the experience, learned something, gained a new perspective, or made new friends through story, could you do us a favor and write a review on Goodreads or wherever you bought the book?

Thanks! We and our authors appreciate it.

We invite you to visit our website, MtZionRidgePress.com, and explore other titles in fiction and non-fiction. We always have something coming up that's new and off the beaten path.

And please check out our podcast, **Books on the Ridge,** where we chat with our authors and give them a chance to share what was in their hearts while they wrote their book, as well as fun anecdotes and glimpses into their lives and experiences and the writing process. And we always discuss a very important topic: *Tea!*

You can listen to the podcast on our website or find it at most of the usual places where podcasts are available online. Please subscribe so you don't miss a single episode!

Thanks for reading. We hope to see you again soon!